The Copper Sands
and
Prince William Sound

By The Same Author

ISLANDS OF EXPERIENCE

A POET'S SKETCH
OF HIS BIOGRAPHY

KID ON THE RIVER

A SAILOR'S YARNS —
AND OBSERVATIONS

TWO CATS FOR PUERTO RICO

THE HIGHLINE TRAIL

ONE LIFE'S THREAD

THE N.P.M.W.A.R.A.
THE NORTH PACIFIC MAJOR WORLD AIR ROUTE AREA

The Copper Sands
and
Prince William Sound

Dean Nichols

Resource *Publications*
An imprint of *Wipf and Stock Publishers*
199 West 8th Avenue • Eugene OR 97401

Resource Publications
A division of Wipf and Stock Publishers
199 W 8th Ave, Suite 3
Eugene, OR 97401

The Copper Sands and Prince William Sound
By Nichols, Dean
Copyright©1994 by Nichols, Dean
ISBN: 1-59752-280-5
Publication date 6/27/2005
Previously published by Binford & Mort Publishing, 1994

For Ramona

"...Lo, they taste the riches of the sea,
and the treasures of the sand."
Deut. 33: Living Bible

Contents

Preface	viii
Prologue	ix
The Call of the Sea	1
Return to the Waters	9
A Slow Beginning	15
An Introduction to the Sands	21
Barney Spielman	29
Shakedown	37
One Eagle Flies	43
A Detective Solves the Case	51
We Sail East	55
A Voyage of Adventure, and Learning	61
The Fish Slimers	71
Prince William Sound, Alaska	79
Problems; the Sands; and History	87
We Voyage West Again	93
The Edges of a Mystery	101
Odd Stories	107
Under The Eye	115
A Fantastic Way to Make a Living	121
Two Nights And A Day	129
Two Stories	133
The Cloak Is Torn Away	139
Plaiting Myself Back Together	147
Eshamy	151

Work—or Play	169
A Fragrant Memory	179
Prologue to Bering River	182
Bering River	183
Epilogue	211

Preface

Although, of course, it is my intention to be as accurate as memory will allow, this is *not* a history book. I ask all, but especially the fishermen of Cordova, Alaska, to be kindly tolerant if they find the name of a person or place misspelled, or even a place misnamed. Rather, this is a reminiscing, a telling to the rest of the world what it was like, 29 years ago, to work and play among a most unique people, and upon the moving waters of the Copper Sands and deep Prince William Sound.

It is also my sincerest prayer that no one named in this book, nor a relative of anyone named in this book will take offense at what is said, or implied about them.

Most assuredly, no offense is intended.

Dean Nichols

Prologue

From my Journal, Anchorage, Alaska, January 24, 1965: "It is the middle of winter, but we had to get out for awhile. We have not been to Seward since that major earthquake nearly a year ago; so we drove the 135 miles south through the snowy mountains.

"When we arrived, although we had read of it in the papers, we were shocked to see the entire dock area gone; and a few damaged piling were all that was left of the small boat harbor.

"However, this was a beautiful, clear, still day, with the mountains competing to show the majesty, strength, and magnificence of their beauty. Resurrection Bay was like a mirror, and that little town as quaint and quiet in its mountain jeweled setting as ever.

"We parked where the ocean dock had once been, ate lunch, and watched the quiet sea with its exciting invitation, calling, and calling, and calling."

This cry burst forth during my long struggle against "the call of the sea" and for remaining with my secure and well-paying job as Air Traffic Control Specialist with the Federal Aviation Agency. I am still glad that I answered that call, and, as my beloved son said, "returned to the waters."

LANDBOUND LAMENT

The sea, the sea, the endless sea
sends out its siren call for me.
Yet oh that call, that haunting call
cannot be heard by one and all,

But only by the hearts attuned
to sense the mysteries it holds,
to feel its healing for my wound,
to hear the challenge to the bold.

A challenge that is not a dare,
but rather invitation there
to see your soul stand tall and free
while held with awe of the endless sea.

March 2, 1964

[From the book, *ISLANDS OF EXPERIENCE* by Dean Nichols]

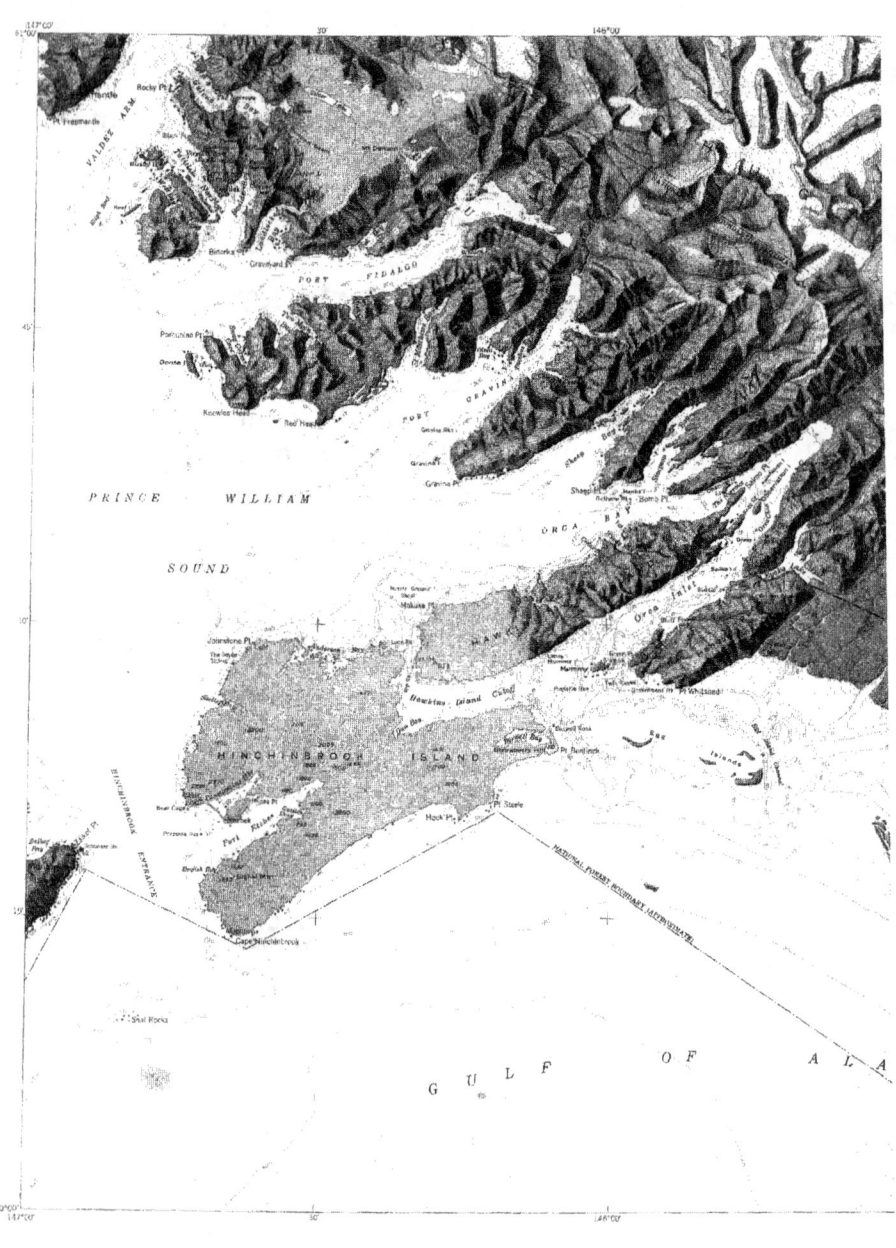

One inch equals about ten miles.

CHAPTER 1

The Call of the Sea

September 20, 1965: The rollers marching in from the Pacific to the south were long and deep, the fathometer swinging from 50 feet in the trough to 65 feet on the crest. The fog had held visibility down to 1 or 2 miles at best for the last several hours, and the low, sandy delta of Alaska's Copper River, with its huge and death-dealing breakers, was invisible in the mist, barely 2 miles away to my right. There was a high chop of 4 or 5 feet running in from the SE at an angle to the rollers, and the M/V *Brant* rolled safely but mercilessly, so that it was a stand-up, brace-yourself ride all the way. The demand was unceasing for close attention to wheel, compass, fathometer, clock and log. I was very literally feeling my way home along the 12 fathom line on the chart.

I was very weary, and my legs were beginning to ache. But I was going home after my longest stay away. The season was ended, and my fascinating job as Protection-Boat Officer for the Alaska Department of Fish and Game would soon be over. But right now, I had several, hard hours ahead of me, and a dangerous, comber-strewn entrance from the sea to make before this voyage was successfully won. And though my surface attention was dominated by the situation at hand, that other part of my mind that psychologists have a name for, was free to review the summer and ponder its value to me in adventure, education, and rich experience.

The wording on this license is no longer allowed by the Coast Guard. But because this is a ninth issue of an original license, the Coast Guard will never reduce the value of the license. *New* licensees will not have the expansive wording. "...upon navigable waters of the United States."

The Call of the Sea

March of 1965: Anchorage, Alaska: And I was completing my seventh year as an Air Traffic Control Specialist for the Federal Aviation Agency. Through long familiarity, the job had become, as jobs sometimes do, routine and confining. This reaction to a really good job was made to stand out in even sharper contrast by the boating magazines to which I had subscribed. They incessantly sang their silent song of the romance of the sea, and reminded me in crystal reverie of those gay and adventurous days as a tugboat skipper on the Columbia River for 20 some years before coming to Alaska.

My increasing voiced discontent with the job at hand, mixed with increasing voiced longing for the waters again, finally drove my wife to suggest, (or was it command?) that I drive out to the Office of the Alaska Department of Fish and Game and see if they had a boat job for me.

The results of that brief interview seemed to startle equally the interviewing officer and myself. Here was just the man they had been searching for as combination Protection Officer (Game Warden) and Boat Officer (Captain) for the patrol boat, *Brant*, out of Cordova. And here was just the job I was looking for, patrolling the fabulous reaches of that mountain-torn sea, Prince William Sound, in a lovely, little ship all my own.

When they first showed me a picture of the *Brant*, a thirty-two foot, fiberglass gill-netter, I looked at her resting against the dock, and it was infatuation at first sight. I had to be her skipper for the coming six-months summer season.

About the middle of April, I took a few days of leave and flew to Cordova (it can be reached only by ferry or plane) one hundred and sixty airmiles SE of Anchorage to look for a house or apartment, meet my new bosses, and see my boat. It was snowing when we landed, and that old DC-3 had to make two passes before getting on the ground. The temperature was around 33 degrees, and slush and mud were everywhere. An old friend who worked for FAA there happened to be across the road at the airport terminal, a small log building, and would be driving in to town shortly, so invited me to ride along.

The 13-mile road, a gravel fill across the soft, delta land, had almost sunk out of sight, and all the several bridges had been destroyed in the 1964 earthquake, so that now the road was under reconstruction with mud, slush, chuckholes, and boulders. The two main streets of the small town, set on the side of a mountain overlooking misty Orca Inlet, were not much better.

When he finally let me out in front of the ancient but freshly painted Windsor Hotel, I thought, with good humor, "What a blazes of an introduction to our new home."

My new bosses were congenial and friendly, and their easy, informal manner, so typical of the culture of a fishing village, made me feel more than welcome. The real shock was housing.

A disastrous fire in 1963 had leveled about two blocks of the downtown section, and a good part of most every building had been old but useable apartments. Nothing more than the introduction of a couple dozen trailers and the building of one modern but expensive auto court had been done since to alleviate the housing shortage.

If my wife and I were "adventurous, and not too fussy," the boys at the office knew of an old and small, but liveable house on piling and attached to an old cannery that was made unuseable by the over 6 foot uplift during the earthquake. They were sure that I could get it rent free for watching the cannery. I couldn't drive to it, but one of the fellows drove me the mile north to the "Ocean Dock", and I walked up the beach for a mile and a half.

The strong and exciting smell of tidelands greeted me, and I was glad. Heavy, wet snow was still falling, although mostly melting as it hit the ground; and there was a light northerly breeze, so that my good wool slacks were getting soaked; I welcomed my snug and warm nylon parka.

It was fun climbing up a rickety ladder and easing myself through a window on the back side. A creek ran between the piling under the attached and partly fallen down shop. The creek served as water supply from up the hill, and sewer outfall to the bay. The house itself was dry and in fair condition; and alone, I had all sorts of fun in my mind, cleaning it up and making it our home of adventure. There was a lovely, old, natural stone fireplace for heating the living room, and an oilstove for heating the rest of the house. Up the ladder stairs in the attic I found two small, neat bedrooms, and on one of the beds a lonely piece of paper carefully laid. The following poem had been waiting for me:

[I publish the following poem without the consent, or knowledge of the author. But she is a fellow poet; she will understand. She had no title; so I have titled it.]

"IN WHAT YEAR?"

"I nestle in your spacious bosom,
                oh mountain towering high.
In your quiet, serene majesty
                you kiss the deep blue sky.
You are so proud, aloof, so haughty;
                through centuries you have ruled
the winds of this deep valley
                where once a tall pine stood.
The deer, the rabbit, the tall pine
                have vanished and been replaced.
But you, cold king of the universe,
                will always be in your place.

                            By D. R.
                          May 15, 1956
                        Cordova, Alaska

Lots of rain and wind today. They had a special clam digger's meeting. We want 15 cents a pound.

            Dorothy Rautio

I am 34 years old. Who will find this? I wonder? In what year?"

I understood her poem—and her questions.

As I walked slowly with the wind back down the beach, spotted with derelicts and pieces of old machinery, and pondered the possibilities of the little house, prudence took charge over adventure, and I realized that the house would not do for us. I would be gone for days and occasionally weeks at a time, and the isolation for my wife there alone would be an intolerable burden. It was too bad. Such charm; such possibilities. It was time to look for my boat.

CHAPTER 2

Return to the Waters

The earthquake had done many strange things. Anchorage, Alaska's largest city, and its environs, and the entire Kenai Peninsula had sunk 3 to 4 feet. Nearly fifty-mile long Montague Island, forming the southern sea barrier for Prince William Sound, had tipped as a stone jostled on a pile of sand, so that one end was shoved up, mountains, beach and

Fishing village of Cordova, Alaska. 1965.

all, an incredible 30 feet. The Cordova area had risen, (according to unofficial but remarkably keen and thereby credible observers) a good 10 or 12 feet, and then settled back, with many accompanying aftershocks, to the official uplift of approximately 6 feet. "The tide just didn't come in for several days," we were told, "and then for a week or two it came in a little farther each day until it settled on a line some 6 feet or more short of its old tide line."

The Cordova harbor was one of the victims of the uplift. At low tide half of it was bare, and the other half was so shallow as to be practically unuseable. Now, over a year later, the slow wheels of reconstruction were turning, and the harbor was a jumble of dredge, pipeline, and equipment, all mixed with boats and floats at anchor in disorganized rafts, seemingly, and often actually, secured almost solely to each other.

Mud, mountains, and an earthquake-injured harbor. Cordova, Alaska. May, 1965.

Alaska State Ferry, M/V *Chilkat*, squeezed in among the "organized confusion" of a hurting harbor during reconstruction. Cordova, Alaska. May, 1965.

I found my way down to the dock, climbed down a 15 foot ladder and out across a temporary ramp in the mud to the nearest flotilla. The downed wires, broken timbers, and general disarray, together with the haphazard collection of boats of all sizes and all conditions, down to actually irreparable derelicts, could have had a destructively depressing affect upon me. But countering that depression was the subtle, yet deep, powerful, and stimulating undercurrent of excitement and expectation, and the definite, though casual preparation for the coming fishing season.

The *Brant* was nowhere in sight, as I ambled down the floats, breathing the aroma of the romance of the sea. I had already been affected by the easy-going attitude of the people. But I knew that I would recognize her at once. I just knew that a ship of her almost haughty personality, character, and breeding would be carefully secured at a berth all her own.

I was mildly shocked to find my little thoroughbred resting patiently amid the pack, the third boat out in a raft of four. Fenders had not been placed between her and the adjoining boats, or they had become dislodged, so that there were ugly scars in what would be lovely, white sides once I scoured off the harbor grime. The radio, mast, rudder, propeller, stack, and other gear were laid about the deck, and, thoroughbred though she obviously was, she was not ready for sea.

The cabin was locked, but a look through the window showed a clean, neat, and orderly combination wheelhouse and galley, with a two-bunk stateroom in the foc'sle. The big after-hatch was unlocked, however, so I lifted it to receive my second series of shocks. The bilge had at least a couple hundred gallons of that mixture of seawater, old oil, and sludge that can only best be described by the use of the lower connotation of the word, bilge. The propeller shaft was disconnected, and on easing myself down into the hold, I received the final blow.

Where the engine should have been, there, in the half-light was a huge, empty space, except for that always seemingly unnecessary maze of disconnected wires, pipes, tubes and belts. Although I had done some major engine repair, and had installed, or assisted in installing a few engines over the years, I did not really consider myself a mechanic; and for a few moments I was stunned by the blow of the problem ahead.

The tide of my enthusiasm for my little ship, and the adventure ahead, was too strong to be deterred by such a small storm, however, so that very quickly I accepted the simple fact that, "Well, if we have to install an engine, then we shall install an engine;" and I walked back up the dock to the Fish and Game Office.

Our search for, and securing of a place to live is a story in itself, but it is really not a part of this story, so let me say only that I found my way to a woman who had a "lovely little trailer house" for rent, paid her three hundred dollars for two months rent in advance, and caught the next plane to Anchorage.

In the course of the following, and all too short days, we sold our snappy, little runabout, hauled loads of junk to the dump, castoff but useable items to the Salvation Army, and other items to the auction. We sold our lovely, big, three-bedroom, full basement, large livingroom-with-fireplace home, and drove our heavily laden station wagon to the sad, depressed and depressing little earthquake-torn town of Valdez. There we boarded the ferry *Chilkat* for the eight, surprisingly rough hours to Cordova, where, during a howling rainstorm, we moved into our tiny, wet, cold and incredibly expensive to heat, 8 x 27 foot "Mobile Home."

During the following two months, this drastic reversal of our living conditions almost became too much for my wife; so that when, two months later, we found what we incongruously came to call our two-story, one-room shack, we could hardly move swiftly enough. The rent and heating and utility costs were less than half, the living area was nearly double, and it was warm and dry. And the view of the harbor below, and the islands and bay were of that priceless and indefineable value. It looked like what it was, an old railroad shack (the basic 10 x 20 unit was built during the 1909 copper mining boom that established Cordova), but we grew to love our simple, little shanty above the sea.

A few weeks after our arrival in Cordova we received a letter from our beautiful son, Lloyd, himself lost at sea a little more than a year later. In his letter, he wrote a poetic expression that deeply touched my heart. He said, "We wish we were there, to share with you your return to the waters. Do you feel as competent as you used to?"

And my answer, "The boat, and area are new and different, and so I have to learn their own, special details and mysteries, but otherwise, it is startling to see myself operating as if I had never left."

So let us now get back to the boats; back to the sea; back to my "return to the waters."

CHAPTER 3

A Slow Beginning

[This is a romantic story of adventure, over dramatically historic waters. I deeply desire to, and believe I shall, present that drama to others. But if some astute readers note a whisper, a very subtle undercurrent of sadness, you will not be wrong. For many seamen, the absence, the long days away, far out upon the waters of this sand and mountain-torn sea, left temptation at home, more than some could resist. Perhaps, perhaps, someday that shall be told. But that part of the story is not for now. This is a romantic story of adventure, over dramatically historic waters. The heroic fishermen of Cordova deserve to have this small part of that story told.]

Here in the South 48, in our urban life, we work, generally, only 8 hours a day. But we do that intensely. Then we rush home intensely, eat dinner intensely, play intensely, even go to bed and make love intensely, and then, because that has become our pattern, we try to sleep intensely, forcing our bodies to accept 6 hours of "intense" sleep in lieu of the 8, or 9, or even 10, that God designed into those bodies.

But there, in that fishing village, clinging comfortably to the side of a mountain, on the edge of the channeled sea, we quickly fell into the slow, uncomplicated pattern of long (10, 12, and often 16 or more hours), easy going, but remarkably productive days. Rarely, I must say, very rarely did urgency become the driving force of any action. As a result, the action flowed easily, and obviously in harmony with the tides in life set by the Master Planner. In the months that followed, I found myself working often 80 hour weeks, even though my pay was for 37½ hours a week. But the thought of complaining never came to mind. I was cruising on a private yacht; and I was being paid for it, and, with all expenses paid. And yet, these two were not the real reasons for those uncomplaining long hours. It was rather that I was happily immersed in a life on the sea; I was in harmony with life, real life.

The training for this easy going lifestyle actually began in Valdez. As in Seward, the earthquake had destroyed all of the docks, so that the state ferry, *Chilkat*, was docking against a temporary, 300-foot, rock-fill mole in the heart of town.

When I checked in at the ferry ticket office (up an outside stairway to the agent's office, which was also her kitchen) and bought our ticket, I found that the "schedule" was *not* for the next day, Monday, but for "sometime" Tuesday, depending on the tide.

We bought our ticket, and walked down to the "terminal," only to find that 300-foot approach and apron (no building) covered by a high tide. And then we understood: Because that temporary landing was built on the shallow delta beach, the ship was able to offload and load vehicles only during a narrow, two-hour time slot halfway between high and low tides. The water had to be down and off that approach so cars could drive there, but not so low that the ferry could not float in the shallow water.

So we got reservations for one more night at the hotel, and I anxiously phoned the Fish and Game Office in Cordova. Rae Baxter, an easy-going biologist, answered. "I'm very sorry," I apologized, "but I cannot make it there tomorrow as we had planned; but will be in on Tuesday's ship."

"OK," Rae answered laconically, "I'll tell somebody, if they're interested."

I puzzled a bit over that response; but in the days to come, I understood.

The ferry, *Chilkat*, was a tubby little thing, about 95 feet long, and with loading and off-loading ramp on the bow only. All 15 cars had to back aboard, so that they could drive forward in debarking. Although her passenger capacity was, I believe, around 52, there were no more than 10 or 15 aboard.

The "restaurant" was also the crew's galley, so once the crew was fed, we had access to it. Once, when we stopped in for something to eat, we found the cook very relaxed under the influence of a liquid other than water. He just waved a hand at the countertop and reefer, and said, "Go ahead and make yourselves a sandwich." We grinned, and did.

But the action station on the ship, the wheelhouse, was also calling. When I stepped in, the highstrung but very able Captain, Don Thornton, was obviously pleased to have the company. And when he found that I was also a boat Captain, he

Although Capt. Dean has been operating boats for over fifty years, it was not until he was age 71 that he decided to go to school and obtain his 100 ton, Master's license. He still occasionally puts it to use.

asked, "Will you take 'er for a little while? I have to get up on the wheelhouse roof and repair an antenna." He gave me the course to steer, and vanished for nearly an hour. I often have since wondered if the Alaska Marine Highway System knows that an old Columbia River towboat man was the sole occupant on the bridge of one of their ships for that hour, out upon that inland sea.

Before the land uplift, from the '64 earthquake, the little *Chilkat* could sneak through the Tatitlek Narrows, behind Bligh Island. But with the level of today's tide, Capt. Thornton didn't want to chance it. There were, as often, however, passengers to board there from the Indian Village of Tatitlek. So he radioed the town, and we hove to for awhile out in the outer bay, lowered the ramp almost to the water, and a skiff came racing out the mile or so from town, and two passengers clambered aboard. The little *Chilkat* plodded on to Cordova. When we finally arrived, no one seemed to be the least concerned that we were a bit late. My pay had begun on May 1st. It was now May 4th.

CHAPTER

4

An Introduction to the Sands

We spent a couple days settling in, and then:

May 6, 1965: Finally to work; that is, doing something to earn my pay. Mechanics from headquarters in Juneau were to be up with the overhauled engine for the *Brant*, in a week or so, so I used the intervening time to study charts and fishing regulations, and to clean up a very sound, but very dirty little ship.

With all the dredging, pile driving, and reconstruction, the harbor was still in an incredible disarray. This time, I had to borrow an outboard-powered skiff, just to get to my craft. But my blood was again being stirred in a way that I had nearly forgotten as I got the oil stove going, a coffee pot on, and began those studies and that cleaning. The sounds of a busy harbor are sweet music to a boat man.

The next day, I took the skiff and made up to the *Brant*, as in old barge-moving days, had fun moving her over to a dock by the ferry slip, and squeezed her in right next to the float, inside three other boats. No one was working on the other three yet, and I wanted to be ready for the mechanics. There was no objection; I was already learning the silent language of the fishermen.

It was even fun scrubbing down that oily bilge with detergent. But the reward came a week or so later, when two mechanics arrived with a spotless engine, and lowered it into that spotless engine room. We were instant friends.

May 10: The 40-some-foot power barge, *Shad*, was taking a crew out to set up markers, east along the Copper River Delta. (The "markers" were approximately three-foot square signs, warning fishermen not to fish "inside" the signs where the restricted waters would give them too much advantage. The signs were nailed to tall poles, set in the sand.)

Capt. Harry Curran, skipper of the *Shad*, had suggested that I go along for a familiarization trip. I wholly concurred and so did my boss, Bobbie Anderson. We left on the tide about 6:30 P.M. for the "flats" and anchored for the night, three hours later, behind the Copper Sands.

Very new "stream guard," Bob Barone, and I had a rich evening, listening to the stories told by Capt. Harry, and by veteran Chief Biologist, Ralph Pirtle. And then we crawled into our bunks; and the roar of the surf a mile or so away, outside the protecting sand bars, the gurgle of water by the hull, the wind, whispering around the warm cabin, the popping of the oil pot on the stove, all in harmony, made soothing music to four sleeping men of the sea.

Tuesday, May 11: Capt. Harry, starting the two 4-53, "Jimmy" diesel engines at an early 6:30, had the rest of us up and dressing. We had, along with the stream markers, 40 or more barrels of gas and stove oil to cache for use by our patrolling cabin skiffs later in the season.

We ran to the head of Copper Slough and rolled off eight barrels of gas and one of stove oil, and *then* we had breakfast.

Two men took two more barrels up the Eyak River in the skiff and cached them. Getting those 300-lb barrels off a boat and up a sandy bank without hoisting equipment, required strength and ingenuity. Pirtle and Curran had both. Barone and I learned.

The Copper River Delta, including the many streams and sloughs, both east and west of the main river, must be fifty miles wide. (Although the term "Copper Sands" did refer to a specific area near Cordova, in this story, I ask the Cordova fishermen to allow me the poetic license to use the term in broad reference, also, to the entire delta and adjoining sands.)

Again, before the 6-foot uplift from the earthquake, most traveling from slough to slough could be done at high tide inside the protecting outer sand bars. But now, to get from one to another, most times required running out into the ocean, and re-entering some miles down. And this we did, heading for Walhalla entrance.

Although I had 20 some years experience running tugs, I had had little experience crossing bars and running in the ocean. I was surprised at how well that low, power barge handled both.

Both because of the curvature of the earth, and the height of the breakers, the low sand bars, marking each side of an entrance, could not be seen soon enough to be used as a guide. Capt. Harry was teaching me, "On this one," he was saying, "you line up the corner of that glacier, with the peak of that mountain, and use that as a range. It will put you right in the middle of the entrance."

There were breakers ahead and for miles each way, as we headed in, but we held to the "range," and in a little while, the surf subsided, and sand appeared both right and left. Quiet water lay ahead.

We anchored a mile or so up the slough and waited for the tide to ebb for awhile. When sand began to appear all around us, we took the skiff, loaded with 16-foot poles, stakes, sledge hammers, shovels and signs, and put up four stream markers. We dug as deeply as we could into the wet sand to set each pole, and then guyed it in place with four wires to the stakes we had driven into the sand. The markers held surprisingly well through the flood tides.

Although Pirtle was the senior officer, he was also a good cook, *and* he enjoyed doing it; so about five o'clock, he prepared an excellent potroast dinner for four hungry men.

No one even thought of "quitting time," so, since it was still daylight, we ran on up the slough a mile or so and off loaded nine more barrels of gasoline for the Walhalla Cache. When we finally anchored up for the night back out by the markers, it was ten o'clock. In my Journal, I noted, "These guys work long hours." I was not complaining, just noting. The innate honesty of these men called them to work (I believe without their putting conscious thought to it) while there was light, while there was work to do.

The short winter days, with their long coffee breaks, in out of the storms, would come soon enough.

Wednesday, May 12: Everywhere, it is sand. And yet, even here, I must speak of the powerful, piercing peaks of Alaska's mountains.

Switzerland has them, Idaho has them, Northwest Washington State has them, all in spectacular array. But nowhere are there so many as in Alaska. Every area of this great land is marked, or framed by mountains, high, stabbing mountains, so steep-walled that often neither snow nor ice can cling to them before the clawing winds. Even out in the broad, flat tundra of NW Alaska, on a clear day, one can look north, or east, or south and see the terrible, towering teeth of real mountains.

And so it was here, on the Copper Sands. I don't think there can be anything more flat than a low sand bar, except the flat water itself; but only a very few miles to the north, the penetrating presence of that towering stone hovered over us; at once awesome and comforting. Awesome with its warning of our puny insignificance, and yet comforting when we know that we walk in the Spirit of He Who made those mountains, and yet Who commanded us to take dominion over the land.

We slept in an hour later, but still, Capt. Harry had us weighing anchor by 7:30 and eating breakfast on the go. He took us again out into the ocean around Grass Island, Kokenhenik bar, and in between Big and Little Softuk, to the confluence of Cudahy Slough, Martin River, and Mirror Slough. Aren't those romantic names?

(I must interject here, that the resident seamen of Cordova were a bit fussy about the correct spelling and the correct pronunciation of those names. A month or so later, I visited a slough back further west, named, obviously, after a man by the name of Pete Dahl. And so, I reasonably reported to Capt. Harry about my visit to Pete Dahl Slough. Capt. Harry Curran, though physically a small man, was a man large in character. He was rarely, and had no need to be, sharp, or harsh with me, or anyone else. But this time, he flung at me the correction, "Peedol Slough," with the accent on the first syllable. I don't remember if I apologized or not, and I felt like someone who had walked into Lovul, Kentucky, and called it Louisville; but I certainly never referred to that slough again, as Pete Dahl Slough.)

But there, high on the sandy bank of the river, or one of the sloughs, we rolled off the remaining 27 barrels of fuel. I don't know if the Fish and Game is still putting out those caches of unlocked barrels in those unguarded places, but then, such was the moral fibre of an otherwise rugged lot of fishermen, that we knew, for anyone to steal any of that fuel would be morally unthinkable. It would be like stealing a man's horse in the early West. It just was not done.

We ran the *Shad* on up Mirror Slough a couple miles and dropped anchor, and Pirtle, Barone, and I rowed ashore, taking axes with us, cut and trimmed 15 more 16-foot poles, and 50 or so 5-foot stakes, and hauled them to the now empty deck of the *Shad*. Cutting and trimming and hauling all those poles and stakes was indeed a full day of work, but obviously, to a small degree at least, even the Alaska Dept. of Fish and Game was "living off the land."

Somewhere in the middle of that hard day of work, we needed a rest, and so did a bit of exploring. Here in this wilderness, we found small, steel rails and railroad spikes. The ties had long since rotted away. But why would anyone build a railroad here? Any reader is certainly free to correct the history here, but as I remember Pirtle's explanation, it was something like the remains of a failed attempt to build a competing railroad to the one that was successfully built from Cordova to the mines, far up the Copper River. Whether that is the true explanation or not, it was startling to see this remnant of history, engraved in steel, here in this lonely place.

As we weighed anchor again, we were poignantly aware of being very tired; but the reward came when we anchored up for the night, about 8:30, back in the deeper water at the confluence of the river and sloughs, and feasted, in that small, warm cabin, on Ralph's choice steak dinner, and fellowshipped, and shared stories of the sea, and of the sands.

CHAPTER 5

Barney Spielman

Early the next day, the sound of an aircraft engine turned our eyes skyward. A Cessna 180, on floats, gracefully circled us and then cut his power, gliding down upon the still waters, and finally drawing those twin feathers upon the silver sea, that only

The M/V *Brant*, haughty Patrol boat for the Alaska Department of Fish and Game, meekly rests among the pack, waiting for her engine. Cordova Boat Harbor. May, 1965.

an expert pilot in a floatplane can do. It was my boss, Bobbie Anderson, and contract pilot, Charlie Allen. I was to fly back with them and complete the readying of the *Brant* for the mechanics. But it also gave me the opportunity to photograph, in my mind, the lay of the bars, and sloughs, and entrances, I would be patrolling in weeks to come. The exposure was very brief, and my mental film not all that fast. Still, the memory is an incredible thing. I was to draw upon that picture many times.

I spent the next two days scrubbing down my little ship, especially that bilge, and then drove out to the airport at mile 13 to pick up the two mechanics from headquarters in Juneau, Ted Bachman and assistant, Merle Brown. I regret now that I did not record more of Ted's jokes. Both men turned out to be remarkably skilled and dedicated mechanics, but Bachman's dry sense of humor kept any problem from ever coming close to being overwhelming.

Though normally a typical, dependable Chevrolet, for some time my old 1962 Chevrolet Station Wagon had, on occasion, refused to start. I loaded their tools; the two men climbed in; I went to start the engine and it wouldn't start. Embarrassed, I climbed out, raised the hood, and made a feeble attempt to locate the problem, probably wiggling a few wires or checking the automatic choke. I heard Merle turn to Ted and ask, "Do you suppose we ought to help him?"

And Ted's spontaneous response, "Now Merle, you know I strained my earballs and can't see a thing without my screwdriver."

Somehow, I did get the engine started, drove them to their hotel, and took their tools down to the *Brant*.

Why anyone would *ever* put a gasoline engine inside a boat is totally beyond me, but the big Marine Conversion of a Chevrolet 409 V-8 arrived the next day, and, working through Sunday, and often ten or more hour days, those two men, over the next four days, had that engine in and running.

I don't know how it is today (how do you write "dedication" into a contract?), but I tell you, back then, I never met a State Employee of the Alaska Dept. of Fish and Game who was not both qualified and able, and truly, truly dedicated. And no one hurt themselves either.

On May 26, 1965, Bobbie asked me to attend an arraignment hearing on Barney Spielman, caught operating an unlicensed skiff. I don't remember how the case came out, but I think that here is the place to interject the story of Barney Spielman.

It is my sincerest prayer that when Barney reads these pages, he will just grin. His name is now going down in history, and will be read of by posterity for many generations.

I believe that he himself will agree that he was a character, a unique character, and thus an excellent candidate for a story.

That he was a tough, very able fisherman, is without question or controversy. And I cannot help but respect Barney, even though his presence among the Cordova fishermen often brought tribulations they and the enforcing officers of the Fish and Game did not need. The storms, the sea, the sand, and tides, and the wrestling with their boats and gear, all these were battle enough.

But, like the mountains to the mountain climber, he was there.

As I said, my first introduction to Barney was at an arraignment hearing for him at the courthouse, for operating that unlicensed skiff. That he hated Bobbie Anderson was openly evident. But I cannot believe that that hatred was of a destructive form. I almost think he needed Bobbie, and the Fish and Game, as antagonists for a driving force within him. It was a kind of game, in which Barney crowded the law, or even stepped over the line on purpose, as quite possibly with the unlicensed skiff, daring someone to catch him. And Bobbie cooperated.

And I don't know whether or not he was the one who wrote those obscenities about Bobbie on the inside of the Cordova jailhouse door, but when we showed them to Bobbie, he very typically burst out laughing.

Bobbie Anderson, himself was a delightfully good-natured young man, and, with a few exceptions, most who knew him loved him. But, he was a native son of Cordova, part Indian, and part Scandinavian. He was gentle and good-natured with that delightful sense of humor. But he was no softie. He could be a formidable opponent, firm, resolved, and right. I am firmly convinced that Barney knew that, and, like the "fast gun" of the old West, couldn't resist the temptation to challenge.

The closest I came to tangling with Barney myself, was near the end of the season, down at Bering River, about 75 miles east of Cordova. I had, by that time, earned some evident respect among the predominantly honest fishermen. A report came to me that Barney was driftnet fishing a few miles away, far up a slough and, of course, well behind the markers. I'd rather not have heard it; I really didn't want to tangle with this able but very tough "fish pirate," as many called him.

So I asked council of several old-timers there. "If I go after him," I said, "I will stir up a lot of trouble; I'll be gone for at least a day from here, and even longer, if we go to court; and, I might not even find him. Yet if I *don't* go, now that I've heard the report, where will my integrity, my authority be with the rest of the fishermen?"

But the council was wise. "Stay here. It's a big stump patch up there; he won't catch that many fish; and besides, he's out of our hair there. We'll respect your authority, Nic."

I knew that they were right. But I also breathed a quiet prayer of thanks.

But there are two more stories that paint more into the picture of this colorful, Cordova character. The well-supported story is that he threw his wife overboard, far out among the sands. It was often told that he and his wife spent many a pleasant evening fighting.

They had been out for two or three weeks, living with a helper, aboard a tiny 20-some foot cabin skiff, or at least a very small boat. The verbal fight was raging. Finally, his wife threw what she thought was a winning blow, "I never get off this boat; I *never* get off this boat."

So, the story goes, Barney decided to give her what she was demanding, "If you want off this boat, get off this boat," and he threw her overboard.

Now before any readers shake their heads in "righteous indignation," I charge you to remember that the rushing tides and the shifting sands, and the often angry sea, demanded decisiveness and swift action of any who would snatch a living from those waters. I just don't buy it that Barney had mayhem at all in mind and would not have, in moments, himself hauled her back aboard. But the story is that his helper reached down over the side, as she drifted past the transom, and hauled her back aboard. But even the most incredulous reader would have to agree; he made his point.

But neither should it be assumed that Barney was not loved. The following story *may* not be about him. But let me tell it; and you decide.

We had moved into that cabin, that "shanty" above the sea. A new tavern had been built at the root of the mole that itself served as roadway to a cannery out by the channel, and as the northern protection for the boat harbor. The tavern had been built for the "convenience of the fishermen," of course.

About 2:00 A.M., one night, my wife, Alma, heard verbal fighting down by that tavern, which was about a hundred feet or so almost vertically below us. She climbed upstairs to look out the kitchen windows to see what was going on. A man and woman were shouting at each other. Women *are* capable of driving men to desperate action, you know, and she was succeeding. Finally, to shut her up, the man grabbed her by the throat; her shouting ceased. In a few minutes, she crumpled to the ground, and he weaved off down the mole toward the boats.

We had no telephone; Alma didn't even know where the single state trooper in town could be found at 2:00 A.M., so for a few moments, she just watched in indecision.

But after a short time, the woman stirred, then sat up, then stood to her feet, and she weaved down the mole, shouting, "Barney, Barney, wait for me."

Alma went back to bed.

That Barney Spielman was a tough, very able fisherman, again, is without controversy. And I believe that he, himself would agree that he was a character, a unique character, and thus an excellent candidate for a story.

The story of the Cordova fishermen would be incomplete without him.

CHAPTER

6

Shakedown

A week or so before that arraignment hearing for Barney, the mechanics had completed the engine installation, and had it running, and so turned the little ship over to me to complete. There was still much to do.

Long, yet fulfilling days followed, getting the radio and mast installed and working, correcting the throttle control, and a water system leak, getting the auxiliary light plant installed, operating and properly covered, the towpost braced and anchored in place (a tugboat man without a towpost?), rigging my anchor and lines, and doing some repair on, and getting my 16-foot, fiberglass, shoreboat ready.

Reference that shoreboat: I was later taught to tow it, out upon the ocean, on a long line astern, to allow for the surge, as the two boats often responded to differing waves. But I didn't like that loose control, especially when running alone, as I often did, so I found some one-half inch nylon line, with its marvelous elasticity, and rigged two eight-foot towing lines in a bridle, one from each corner of the transom to the towing ring on the bowstem of the skiff. The elasticity of that nylon took the shock of the occasional jerking, and, I had close control. A small airplane tire, fastened around the point of the bowstem, took care of the rare times that it bumped the stern of the *Brant*.

I don't know if I just "lucked out" or not, but over the ensuing months, I made some mighty wild entrances and exits through those breakers, down along the Copper Sands, and only once took a little water aboard that skiff.

No one even suggested commercial fenders, and a towboat man without adequate fenders... Well... So I went out to the city dump and found four, white sidewall tires, and mounted two on each side, 10 or 12 feet apart. Except in rough water, they stayed right there, and actually added to the *Brant*'s haughty, black and white Police Boat look. They also made for easy, snappy landings alongside docks or other boats.

A single piece of small, nylon line, secured on a cleat amidships, also facilitated snappy securing of her alongside that dock or other boat... Springlines and fore and aft breast lines could be added later, if needed. A typical single-screw displacement boat, she pulled left when backing down; and that meant that, whenever possible, we made a port landing, often quite impressive. And, it was fun.

Over the years, I've concluded that 80 percent of the men who run boats, just run them, apparently having no interest in developing real skills in that marvelous challenge of boat handling. The next 10 percent handled boats with *some* evident skill. But the last 10 percent handled boats with a flare, an obvious desire to always improve, to make them dance upon the waters. I wanted always to be in that top 10 percent; and that marvelous little ship cooperated fully.

Even the propeller and shoe had been removed for repairs, so finally I got the *Shad* to tow us a few miles to the New England Cannery at Orca, where we lifted my boat out and onto a cradle on the dock. I didn't like at all the way the shoe mounted. If one ran over an anchor line, it would definitely hang up on the protruding portion of the shoe. But I had no choice; and then reminded myself, "I'm not tending a dredge on the Columbia River. We'll not be running over any anchor lines." So I bolted that otherwise beautiful bronze into place.

It was a cold, rainy, stormy evening when I finally got my little ship back into the water, back home in the bosom of the sea where she belonged, and took my "maiden voyage," back to Cordova, alone. My Journal for that day records only one word, "Good." But it was much more than that; my soul had finally been re-united with the Spirit of the sea, and the resonance sang its silent yet lovely song. I *knew* I was in perfect harmony with the will of He who had put me there.

Of course we had to take a few, short, "shakedown" cruises; so when, the next evening, Bobbie Anderson, and contract pilot, Charlie Allen, asked me to take them on a short run, I happily complied. They wanted to check their crab pots. But when we pulled them, we found no crabs. So we ran on up to Salmo Point, and lifted several that had been set by commercial fishermen, and got about 20, beautiful, huge, Dungeness crabs.

When I questioned Bob about the pulling of someone else's pots, he reassured me, "Oh, they really don't mind, as long as we re-bait the pots." Later, other fishermen told me, "Sure, pull a few pots, if you need to. And if you don't have any bait, why, just leave a jug, or a six-pak in there. We'll understand."

Before that season, that marvelous adventure, was over, I had learned a quiet, but fascinating characteristic of those fishermen; a characteristic that I am sure, most were not even aware of themselves. There was so much bounty in the sea, that they had a gentle, but very real need to give some of that bounty away. Many times I would be hailed, or one would swing alongside, and they would give me a small halibut that had been caught in their salmon net, or some Tanner crabs that had been caught in their Dungeness crab pots.

A medium sized king crab. A gift from a fisherman.

No, this was in no way at all, an attempt at bribery. They just had that deep, inner need to give away a portion of the bounty of the sea; and I was there.

The next day, Sunday, I took one more "shakedown cruise," and took my wife, and Border Collie pet, Cindy, up to Orca to show the New England Cannery, back down to Odiak Channel, and then up to Salmo Point, where we pulled a crab pot for a few crabs, and a flounder. A pair of "killer" whales were cruising there, so we shut the engine down so we could hear them blow, not 50 feet away. That dog nearly went wild as she apparently heard some message of challenge from those animals of the sea. Obviously, the massive size of those monsters was not evident to her, or she would have been properly cowering below decks.

But enough of preparing, enough of shakedown cruises and training. The season was beginning. There was real work to do.

CHAPTER 7

One Eagle Flies

The season was rapidly coming on, with the harbor quite literally humming with preparation. We were completing our own preparations, and as I walked down the floats one day, an Indian crew, sitting, and lying up on their piles of nets on the deck of their fine looking, 40-foot purse seiner, were very drunk. As I passed by, an old, white fisherman, obviously also an old friend, called them down, "It's time for you guys to sober up; you've a lot of work to do, and the season opens in two weeks."

The Captain grunted some response, and their friend walked away. I don't know the result of the exchange; but the Indians were normally excellent fishermen, so they probably responded. There clearly was no racial prejudice in Cordova, or certainly none that I saw. Since, however, the terrible divisiveness of the so-called, "Native Land Claims Settlements" in Alaska, things may have changed, but back then, we were obviously all one as God meant for us to be.

But that drinking. Maybe I'm just a little prejudiced in favor of these unique people, the Cordova fishermen, but I just don't believe that that bottle ruled them, or, rarely, as in the case of a story that follows, if it did, they had someone to lead them back to productivity. Many, if not most, drank much during the long winters. But when the seasons opened; their consciences demanded that they cork the bottle, and they did. And then they threw *all* of their energies into their boats and nets, and in pitting their skills against the bounty laden, yet often angry sea.

There were probably others, but I knew of one, quite successful fisherman who had to be the conscience for his wife and their able deckhand. As I remember the story, the Captain did not drink much, if at all, but this otherwise fine woman and that otherwise able deckhand would spend much of the winter in the bars.

Spring came, and it was time to begin preparations for the coming fishing season. The Captain went to the bar and told the two truants. They were jovial and agreed. The Captain went down to their boat and continued with the work of preparation. The truants continued with their drinking.

Daily the tug-of-war waged; and the Captain completed his preparations alone. Finally, it was time to sail. The Captain bought the most expensive bottle of whiskey he could find, took it to his two "children," and told them, "I'm taking this down to the boat to open. If you want to share, come on down."

The temptation was too great. They followed him, or that bottle, to the boat. Getting them comfortably settled in the galley, with glasses and that jug, the Captain quietly slipped his lines, started his engine, and ran from the dock. When the bottle was finished, and the two sobered up, they were well out upon the sea. And then the two became what they truly were, an able deckhand-fisherman, and an able, caring wife whose immaculate ship, and fine food were known throughout the fleet.

From my Journal, May 30, 1965: "Ran [the *Brant*] up to the Standard Oil Dock this morning, to fuel up, and load a barrel of outboard motor gas aboard. How fulfilling it was there, with the throb of activity, with several large tenders refueling, plus dozens of boats, larger, and smaller than the *Brant*, coming and going. [The "tenders" were most often, large power barges, with the capacity to anchor for some time in one place, far out in some fishing area, and buy fish from the many small fishing boats, who could not economically run back "home" with every catch of fish.]

"...A real storm developing, so Bob and I worked inside on the *Brant* all afternoon, getting a balky bilge pump going, doing several of those last minute chores that nag every preparation for sea, and, of course, taking those necessary coffee breaks around the galley stove, listening to the storm, and telling jokes with Charlie Allen, and John David Solf, summer biologist..."

In my book, *A POET'S SKETCH*, there is a story, "Cordova Boat Harbor." In the story, there is a short, but poignant portion telling about this most unique man, John David Solf. I shall not repeat it here; but I can say without apology that for any to miss that brief story of John David is to miss touching a treasure; just touching, but a touching that will enrichen lives.

F. M. J. Monday, May 31, 1965: "We left Cordova on the late morning tide, towing my skiff, and the Cabin Skiff, *Stingray*, with Bobbie Anderson and Deputized Protection Officer and *Stingray* operator, Jerry Baron aboard... Bit foggy, but across the "flats," and anchor up behind the Copper Sands in late afternoon for lunch... Later, the fog lifted, so we ran up to the Copper barrel cache, to show Jerry his fuel base and to anchor up for the night. We are losing oil in the reverse gear, and gaining in the engine... It looks bad..."

The *Stingray* was a wooden, flat-bottomed, 20-some foot skiff, with a pair of about 30 or more hp outboard motors mounted on the stern. Just ahead of the motors was a tiny cabin, not more than 5 by 7 feet, a single bunk, two-burner Coleman gas stove, food, probably a 5 gallon bucket for a sink, and another for a head (toilet). It was just about the ultimate minimum that one could call living quarters; but, if one compared that with living out under the stars—and the fog, and the wind, and the rain—then that tiny, tiny cabin could be a real haven, or even heaven, at times.

I know that we had two, and maybe three of these "bow pickers," as they were called. We used them strictly for patrol craft, but they were called "bow pickers," because the forward half or two-thirds of the boat was open, so that, when used for fishing, the fisherman could have room to work, room to pile his nets, and, being away from the propellers, could haul his nets aboard over the bow without entangling those nets in those propellers.

Jerry Baron, himself, was, I believe, a New York boy. I don't think he had ever been on, or at least had never run a boat in his life. He had just answered the "Ad," and applied for the job of "Stream Guard," or "Stakeout crew." But he was obviously sharp, thoughtful, a ready learner; so we made him a "Cabin Skiff Patrolman."

"I haven't the slightest idea of what I'm supposed to do," he protested.

But Bobbie answered in that good-natured way that just dismissed any reason for anxiety, "Oh, don't worry about it, Jerry, we'll teach you." And we did.

He was an excellent choice; he learned readily, and well. And, as an added bonus to the Dept. of Fish and Game, he had, we found, an innate diplomacy, and a firmness, that, together, made him both liked and respected by those rugged fishermen.

The general purpose for this first patrol was for Bob to teach Jerry, and me, about checking boats and fishermen for licenses and filling out the proper forms. And he taught us how to spot possible departures, or potential departures from the "rules;" such as spotting unlicensed children helping with the gear, how to sight across the sands to the next marker to see if a boat is "crowding the line." He taught us how to watch the lay of a boat in the water that might indicate a load of fish, illegally caught in the night, and other skills of patrolling. For all this schooling, though, there was still some time for play.

Bob had mentioned something like, "I suppose we ought to dig a few clams."

"YOU mean, there are clams around here?" Jerry asked, incredulously.

"Oh, sure," Bob had assured him, "Right over there on that bar. We'll dig some tomorrow morning on the low tide."

We were up the next morning by 4:00 A.M., and ran to Johnson Hole.

I was fortunate, on most of my trips that year, to have a good cook on board, and one who liked to cook. Bobbie was one; and in that tiny wheelhouse-galley he soon had three hungry men at a tiny table, feasting on a giant's breakfast.

I soon found that I didn't like having anyone else cleaning up my galley; you know how it is, they *never* put things away in the right place. So while I cleaned up, Bob grabbed a clam shovel and took Jerry in the skiff over onto that now exposed sand bar. In 30 or 40 minutes they were back aboard with 2 or 3 dozen huge razor clams. While they cleaned clams, I worked on my ailing engine, and then we did some more work on the art, and it was that, of being a Protection Officer for the Alaska Dept. of Fish and Game.

Lunch time came around, and of course, we must have a clam feed. As that aroma like no other wafted out of that small galley, the radio crackled. Charlie Allen, in the floatplane, was calling base and gave his position. We spotted him, 8 or 10 miles northeast of us, over against the mountains. So we called him, and invited him to the clam feed.

Sure," he radioed back, "but where are you?"

We told him, but he still could not see us. Once in a while, on the silver sea, the reflections from the sky will almost hide a white boat, so we understood. So we radioed back, "Just do as you're told, Charlie, turn left about 45 degrees."

He did. We watched a bit, then gave a minor correction, then, "You're coming right for us, Charlie."

"OK," he answered, "But I still don't see you."

When he was less that 1 or 2 miles away, we told him, "Just trust us, Charlie, cut your power and start letting down."

He was less than half a mile away, when, like seeing suddenly the picture in an optical illusion puzzle, the *Brant* was there. He made his feathery landing, taxied up, and we caught a line. He was just in time for dinner.

There are strange things seen, and hidden, out upon the waters. Sometimes the currents, together with light breezes, will lay straight streaks upon that illusory mirror. And with the dark sand nearby adding its confusion, the *Brant*, pointed directly toward him, just blended with those streaks and lines, and sands.

Finally, we pushed Jerry, the baby eagle, off the limb. "Go check a few boats," we told him; "Try your wings. You are far more able than you might think." And he was, and he flew.

Bob flew back to Cordova with Charlie, and I limped back across the shallow, uncharted "flats" with my ailing little ship. I was just a little disappointed; yet, years upon the waters had told me, animals get sick, people fail us, machinery breaks down. So, we make the repairs, and go on. The M/V *Brant was* a fine, seaworthy, very real little ship. This eagle too, shall fly.

CHAPTER 8

A Detective Solves the Case

Quiet, but very personable mechanic, Merle Brown flew back up again from Juneau to help me find and correct that oil problem. It was good to see him again. Life has a curious way of just giving us glimpses of people who might otherwise become close friends. Although I never saw Merle or Ted Bachman again after the rich adventure of that summer, I have always regretted that I could not have known them better.

Although many readers may not be deeply interested in the mechanics of engine repair, I know that many readers will themselves be either mechanics, or boatmen, or both; and so will appreciate the detective job Merle had to do to find the trouble.

That reverse gear (transmission) coupled closely to the engine used the same kind of 30-weight engine oil as the engine, but did not share the *same* oil. There was a seal around the shaft to prevent any mixing. But as I've said, by measuring both, we knew oil was moving from the gear to the engine.

The gear had been overhauled in Juneau the previous winter, but—that oil.

That gear must have weighed 50 to 75 lbs, so it took some doing to get it all unbolted, lifted out of place, and opened up so we could look for the trouble. It was work, and it was delaying my job of patrolling. But, there just is something fulfilling about working in the dry, in the tiny cabin of a boat, with the sounds of the sea and a busy harbor about.

Over the next two days we had that gear out, torn down, reassembled, and reinstalled, two or three times; and each time, one or two hour test runs were made. On a beautiful test run up to Shepard Point and back, I traded, at Merle's suggestion, an outboard motor generator I'd found to a fisherman for two beautiful sockeye salmon; so we had a feast that night.

Finally, the detective in that skilled mechanic deduced what the trouble had to be, and he was right. Although a new seal had been installed between the gear and the engine, the repairman had missed an almost imperceptible groove that the original seal had worn in that smooth shaft. It is nearly impossible to set a new seal exactly to fit that tiny groove, and he had missed by a minute fraction of an inch. That left the seal very slightly out of square with that groove. The "wobble" of that groove under that new seal worked as a very minute but incessant pump, pumping a fraction of a drop of oil from the gear to the engine each revolution. There were over 2000 revolutions every minute. In a couple hours or so, it added up to that quart or more of oil.

Merle simply drove the seal in another one-eighth of an inch or so, so that it had its own, perfect, smooth area of shaft, and the problem stopped. I still believe that gasoline engines do not belong in boats; *but*, that *was* a Chevrolet. The rest of the season, it performed faithful to its heritage.

CHAPTER

9

We Sail East

F. M. J. June 6, 1965: "A real storm all day. Checked with Bob. Ralph Pirtle wants to go east to check reports of downed markers. But a call for weather forecast found winds of 35 to 50 knots. Harbor is a good place to be; we shall sail tomorrow... Up to the 'cabin,' and hauled loads of ____, ____, and corruption out... Really stormy tonight."

We had contracted to rent that "shanty above the sea," but were paid up where we were to the end of the month, so we used the intervening time to clean up an incredibly filthy dwelling. It was almost unbelievable that human beings had lived there.

As we worked, and cleaned, and hauled those loads of refuse to the dump, we were unaware that *any*one was watching, or caring. But such is the character of this small village, that the entire fishing community knew, and were impressed. That impression was to have its influence in making my exercising of authority much more harmonious over the next several months.

There was not even a latch of any kind on the door, so I rigged a simple wooden bar to turn in place. Alma mildly complained to Biologist, Rae Baxter, who, with his wife and beautiful little girl, owned the nearly identical shanty, 6 feet over from ours, "We can't even lock our door," she told Rae.

Rae looked at her in surprise, "Why would you want to lock your door?"

And he was right. Over the months that followed, we found that if she chose to be, a woman was safer on the streets of Cordova at 2:00 or 3:00 in the morning than on the streets of Anchorage at noon day. Some chose not to be; but no one was forced in the gentle culture there. The sea was challenge enough.

The next day, we loaded Ralph's gear aboard, I shopped for groceries and stowed them aboard. The Department had a specified food allowance of, I believe, $1.09 per man/meal. I was later to discover that the other boats always ran way over; but, because I bought much less meat, mine ran way under. So, I concluded, there should be *some* compensation. So after that, when I bought groceries for the ship, I included enough for home. And still my expenditures were under that allotted $1.09.

Oh, of course, I wouldn't do a thing like that today, and it was without doubt, illegal as could be, but the rationalization isn't *too* faulty. I think it is a good thing, however, that the Statute of Limitations has run out.

And speaking of "technically" illegal things: Later in the season, summer-hire, Dick Smeltzer, brought us some ducks he had shot; and later, some more. We really appreciated that, of course, but shotgun shells cost money; so we bought him shells. He enjoyed the hunting; we enjoyed the meat; it seemed like a good deal, until another fine biologist, and good friend, Loyal Johnson, reminded us that that exchange was illegal. So we stopped—talking about it. But back to the Copper Sands.

Again, F. M. J., Tuesday, June 8, 1965: "...Left Cordova on the tide at 6:30 P.M. with Ralph Pirtle aboard, and anchored in Johnson Hole about 9:30. We ran over in our skiff to visit Jerry Baron in the *Stingray*."

In that one week, that young man had begun to establish himself with those fishermen, and in his own mind. As I too was to learn, there was no way under the sun that we could be a Police *Force*, but had, instead, to rely on the cooperation of the 90 percent honest, and the fairly honest fishermen. We just did not have enough eyes.

The honest fishermen wanted to play it honest; but with no "law" around, it would be awfully hard to *not* start early, or fish late, or fish inside the markers, while some other boat was doing so, and, getting away with it. With one of us somewhere around, then the honest ones could say, "Hey Joe, you'd better not do that; the Fish and Game isn't that far away." And it worked. We really were all in this together.

I don't know how it is today, but then, many fishermen told me that they were *much* happier with the State Fish and Game than they had been with the Federal Fish and Wildlife Service before Statehood. "Under the 'Feds' we almost lost the

Fishery," they told me. "Now, the State is bringing it back. That is good for all of us."

For some reason, I had very little contact with another Biologist, Bob Roys. He seemed to keep to himself. But he had developed a keen, almost prophetic skill at forecasting the actual number of salmon we could expect each coming season. I believe they would do such things as going out after the spawning, and digging in the gravel over a specific number of square feet or yards, and count the number of live eggs. Over the very few years that the State had had control, they had developed a fair estimate of the total number of square yards over an entire spawning area. Using that data, nebulous as it might have been, and adding in factors of weather and past runs, and finally adding in that really nebulous factor of intuition, he was repeatedly amazingly close in his estimates each year. The fishing periods were thus increased or decreased in each area, so that enough salmon made it to the beds to spawn, and thus build or at least maintain the fishery. As I said, I hardly knew him, but my memory reminds me that Bob Roys was a respected Biologist. I think that is good.

And all these things added together to make Jerry's and my job of enforcing the law, *so* much easier.

But there was still another factor, the quiet man aboard my ship, Ralph Pirtle. As I understood it, he was *not* the "head of the Fish and Game in Cordova." For example, the Protection Division, represented there by Bobbie Anderson, and myself and others, were really not under his authority. But there was something about this quiet man that drew us all to look to him, at least for counsel, if not actual direction.

And yet, on this voyage, as we cruised the silver sands and the stormy sea, he was a real companion. We worked some very long days at times but as I've said before, we really didn't notice. Tomorrow, if the storm will allow us to, we sail east again, skirting the shallow sands.

CHAPTER
10

A Voyage of Adventure, and Learning

Bastendorf Beach, The Oregon Coast, February 22, 1989: As I sit here writing, in the snug comfort of my modern Coachman Travel Trailer, I am "at anchor in a protected cove." The wind is more than sighing through the evergreen trees up on the hill, it

The author in the "snug comfort of his travel trailer," remembers, and writes of, another storm of long ago.

is rushing through with a noisy blast that warns of its terrible power. The white surf, with its seeming incongruity of ordered confusion, pounds and claws at the yielding yet eternal sands, less than half a mile away.

The sun is shining now, in that brilliant intensity that comes after the washing of the rain; for a cold front has just passed through. But in passing, through the night and early morning, it poured out its own fury in such volume that this tiny cabin shook as if being slammed by the weight of a dozen waterfalls. And the voice of that falling water, for just a little while, drowned out the voices of even the blasting wind and the pounding sea.

And I, I who have known the terror of the storm at sea, sit quietly before the fire in my snug little cabin, in a protected cove, and revel in the security of my fortress.

And I remember back to a different time, nearly a quarter of a century ago, when my "Cabin" was that of a 32 ft, Bristol Bay Gill-netter, and my "fortress" was a shallow cove protected by the quiet strength of the Copper Sands.

F. M. J., Wednesday, June 9, 1965: "We were up at 5:30, and pulled out for Grass Island. It was my first experience at slamming that little ship through such heavy breakers. I learned much respect for and confidence in the seaworthiness, the just plain toughness of my little ship. But I learned also, as we cleared the shallow entrance and steadied down in the open sea, that, though we had won, we had done so over a formidable opponent.

"But even in the open sea, there was a SSE swell of 6 to 10 feet, with an ESE mean chop of 3 to 4 feet on top. But suddenly, I felt at home. I had battled the same stormy waves as a tugboatman on the mighty Columbia River for many years, and had found that, with a well-designed, well-built craft, and a prudent Captain at the helm, though the storm at sea could put up a wearying fight, it could be beaten.

"But those breakers on entering and leaving those shallow entrances... Those breakers, that had, over the years, taken the lives of even some mighty men of the sea, they demanded and received my deep respect.

"We entered through the wild breakers again, and arrived in the quiet water behind Grass Island three and a half hours later. Breakfast, finally, and then we took the skiff and ran out and put one downed marker back up, straightened up another, and checked several more.

"It was really quite stormy, so we just holed up for a few hours. But impatience, that which has carried good men to their destruction before us, nudged us; so we weighed anchor about 5:00 P.M., and thrust back through the slamming breakers, heading for Softuk.

"The SSE swells were now up to 8 to 10 feet, with an ESE sea of 4 to 6 feet on top. It was just plain rough, mean rough."

[During my entire summer, cruising that northern edge of the Gulf of Alaska, it was always rough. Sometimes more rough. Sometimes less rough, but always rough. Old time fishermen I talked to agreed, yes that *is* the North Gulf Coast. "However," one veteran told me one day, "I have actually run all the way across the Gulf of Alaska with two boats tied side-by-side."

But for my year there, that was not to be. I was increasingly grateful that I was riding that well-designed, well-built, floating challenger of the free and wild sea.]

Continuing from my Journal: "We found the Softuk can (buoy) had drifted west one to two miles, so we lined up a couple mountain peaks, and, with Ralph's 'local knowledge,' crashed our way in through the Softuk entrance, and anchored up in Coffey Hole about 8:00 P.M.... Fisherman, Leonard Wheeler, gave us a beautiful Sockeye salmon."

F. M. J., Thursday, June 10, 1965: "I really slept in, for a change, till nearly 8:00 o'clock. But that always new and tantalizing aroma of hotcakes, bacon and eggs cooking, and coffee simmering on the stove, brought me, awake and grinning, up into the galley. Maybe the sea gave us a special appetite, but that Pirtle is a good cook.

"The storm is down; a glorious day... Pirtle took the skiff over for a visit with the boys on the *Montague*, Rae Baxter's larger cabin skiff from which he does much of his research. I worked on my boat a few hours, repairing a shift mechanism and tuning up other parts of the machinery that together make a boat a whole...

"This evening, I hooked my outboard motor on, with the one there, on the *Baracuda*'s skiff, and, racing like a sea sled, cruised the fleet, and up into Mirror Slough, mostly making my presence there known. As I've said, that was really about all the honest fishermen asked."

F. M. J., Friday, June 11, 1965: "Charlie Allen dropped from the sky about 10:00 A.M. Pirtle was needed for some business back in Cordova... I took the big skiff again, cruised the fleet, and checked licenses on a few boats. That big, flat bottomed, Cordova skiff would do 20 to 30 miles per hour with those two motors. Standing up, fisherman style, to steer, and with the wind in my face, it felt, I think, as a hang glider would feel; that is, as close to flying as man could be. A simple, flat-bottomed fishing boat; but it flew. This afternoon, another cruise of the fleet, and then 'home' for the day about 5:30... Old man Coffey gave me a 30 lb halibut... A beautiful day."

The bounty of the sea.

I would like to know more of the story of "Old man Coffey." And maybe, someday, someone will write of him. But as I remember, he was white-haired, white-bearded, and very much the picture of the "Old man of the sea." Quite possibly, Coffey Hole was named after him—or his father—or his grandfather. And I don't know how old he was, but certainly in his seventies, or possibly eighties. He fished alone, but cautiously, and, I understood, with reasonable but steady success. When he gave me that fish, I really sensed a Spirit of warmth and kindness and a very subtle amused confidence flowing from him.

"Oh, that fresh, fresh halibut was good. But I was increasingly becoming aware of an almost indefinable something else that was happening. The richest food I was receiving from that bountiful sea was the food of the Spirit, a food that was coming to me from the spirits and souls of those men who had so become a part of that life-giving sea."

F. M. J., Saturday, June 12, 1965: "Up at 7:45 to catch the Marine Forecast on the radio. ESE winds, 15 to 25 knots, they said... Wrote a letter home, and packaged up most of that salmon and halibut, to send in with Charlie when he brought Pirtle back out at 11:00... [After he arrived] we ran up to Mirror Slough for a couple hours, waiting on the tide, and cut a few more poles and stakes, then back to Softuk and took the skiff out in the blustery wind and rain, and put some downed markers back up...

"We found a half dozen or so, large and live crabs, caught in a portion of net that had hung up on one of the markers. The sea keeps giving. Pirtle's talents continued to emerge, as he quickly, and deftly cleaned those crabs...

"It was really rough at the Softuk entrance, so we ran back to Coffey Hole for the night and feasted on a crab salad one could not buy... The wind is crying around the cabin at 30 to 35 knots tonight."

F. M. J., Sunday, June 13, 1965: " 'Six days thou shalt labor, and the seventh...' Well, we shall rest, when we get home... A beautiful day. We were up at 4:30 to catch the low tide and put up a pair of markers. Back for breakfast, and a visit with fisherman, Bud Oldham, and then we pulled out for Bering River on the flooding tide about 9:00. The storm had quieted, so we had an easy, clear ride down, and were anchored inside before noon... Another incredible crab salad for lunch. (What incongruity. We were dressed for the sea, and the storm, and the sand; and yet we were feasting better than ones dressed for 'dinner' at Ivar's in Seattle.)

"We took the skiff, and set up the two Bering River Markers and had a visit with the skipper of the purse seiner, *Pam*. It was glassy calm, and beautiful... About 9:30 P.M., on the high tide, and well before dark, the *Pam* suggested we follow him around the north side of Kanak Island to the east anchorage. He must have drawn a foot or two less water than we. We followed, and wallowed around for an hour and a half, and finally gave up and anchored back where we were about 11:00 P.M... That earthquake uplift had driven us to the open sea again."

F. M. J., Monday, June 14, 1965: Bob and Charlie Allen flew in about 2:00 A.M. We wouldn't get up, but just told them to fix their own breakfast... We did get up about 5:00, though, and saw them off on Aerial Patrol, and then, with that low tide, we took the skiff, and a pair of clam shovels, to an outer bar, and dug 40 or 50 lbs of razor clams... We will take them back for distribution among the Fish and Game family. That was just understood... A Cordova Airlines amphibian brought in two 'Stakeouts,' Rick Petri, and Dennis Rae. We put them ashore, and helped them locate a good campsite..."

[Although we couldn't do it this time, normally we tried to slip a 'Stakeout' crew into place in the night, so that no one knew where we did, and did not have those hidden eyes. The main purpose for the 'hidden' crews, was simply that we did not have the manpower to cover *all* of the areas where fishermen might be tempted to net the schooling salmon just inside the markers. So, at least in theory, they did not know where a Stakeout Crew might be hidden. I think it worked, to a degree, but nothing could do better than the simple honesty of those "90 percent."]

"...We finally pulled out for the east side (of Kanak Island) about 6:00 P.M. A lovely, quiet day, and ride. Wingham Island, a mile or so off shore, and looking more like a misplaced, South Sea Island movie set, was beautiful in the late afternoon light.

"The east entrance was amazing. There was *no* bar, *no* breakers. The sea swells just slowly subsided until we were a mile or so inside, in quiet water. I checked it out in my copy of the *Coast Pilot*. Apparently, the scouring tides had kept the entrance very deep for many, many years. I read that even sailing ships had found a hole they could run for, even during a gale, and safely enter for protection from the storm.

"We were anchored down in that historic place by 7:30. This is the very eastern end of my 'beat.' I sense some mystery, some message of history, drifting with the gentle breezes tonight."

F. M. J., Tuesday, June 15, 1965: "We were up at 6:00, and put up two more markers. Breakfast, and then pulled out about 9:00... We picked up trapper, Charlie Boyd, pigtail hair, aluminum canoe, and gear, and headed home on almost glassy rollers... We anchored off Fox Island, and took the skiff ashore, and explored for an hour or so. What a fascinating place, with thousands of Murrelets, Seagulls, and other birds. And, we found more railroad rails, up on the flat top of this vertical walled island. What is the story that that mute steel could tell?...

"We had intended to go only as far as Softuk, or Grass Island, this day; but the weather was good, with a following sea, so we decided to run on in. It got pretty sloppy, by the time we made Strawberry Entrance, and the blowing sand was pretty thick, but we made it OK, and were safely at the dock in Cordova by 8:30... It has been a long, but interesting day; and a voyage of rich adventure and learning."

CHAPTER

11

The Fish Slimers

The Spirit Of Harvest

[This story is in no way whatsoever meant to impugn the character of anyone. The Cordova fishermen, male and female, were colorful characters, and, like Barney Spielman, were thus excellent candidates for stories.]

"Can I *what?*" was my wife, Alma's unintended, but spontaneous response to the question.

There was silence on that telephone for a moment, perhaps a sigh, and then, with just a bit of irritation, the woman on the other end repeated, "Can you slime fish?"

Alma may not have been a super intellect, but she certainly was no dumbbell, and, she could think on her feet. She had called the office of the cannery, out on the "Ocean Dock," just north of town, for a job.

She was not one to be idle, and, with no children at home, and a voyaging boat Captain for a husband, she needed something to give her energies to.

She realized that that brief exchange on the phone had left her just a bit off balance. So she stepped back, caught her balance, and came in again. She knew, of course, if it was a job other women could do, she could do it too.

"I'm sorry," she corrected, "I don't know for sure what you are talking about. But if it has anything to do with cleaning fish, yes, I have cleaned hundreds, over the years; I'm not afraid of work and, I can learn. My husband is Captain of the Patrol Boat, *Brant*, and will be gone much of the time; I need something constructive to do while he is away."

Whether or not that last had any influence, we don't know, but the hint of a smile came over the phone, "Aw, come on over and sign up. I think we can put you to work." And they did.

The "slime line," was a moving conveyor belt about waist high, carrying the salmon that had just come through the "Iron Chink." The "Iron Chink" was the admittedly uncomplimentary name given to the machine that had come to replace the Chinese workmen who for years had cleaned the fish before the canning process began. Like all machines, it could not think, and like most machines, although it worked tirelessly, and much more swiftly, and at far lower cost than man, it left an imperfect product that only the human mind, and human hands could complete. Thus, the slime line.

There were, I believe, about six or eight stations along the slime line. At each station was a heavy block of wood, or cutting board, a large, razor sharp butcher knife, and about a half inch stream of cold water pouring down upon that board. As the fish came down that belt, the women would grab one, and with that knife, scrape off any excess slime, trim any fins left hanging, and scrape out any remaining entrails that the Iron Chink had missed, and quickly rinse off the fish.

Although those women wore warm clothing, and a heavy, full length, waterproof apron, it was hard, repetitive, fatiguing work that, curiously, I believe a man could not endure as well. The Good Book is correct in referring to women as "the weaker vessel," that is, in an active, battle sense. But when it comes to just hanging in there and enduring, and not giving up, my years of observation have given me to determine that women have the edge on us men.

That is not to say that those women did not become very, very weary, standing there for, I believe, eleven hours a day; and Alma admitted to me that she very nearly quit several times. As I recall, they began work at 7:00 A.M., and worked until 8:00 P.M., with four, half hour rest and coffee or lunch periods spread through the day, two or three hours apart.

Alma herself had inherited an iron constitution from her French Canadian mother, and her indefatigable German father. Life, the Bible says, and science is confirming, is in the blood. Alma died of leukemia in 1983. When the death angel attacks the blood, that life, then all that iron constitution, all that inherited reserve of energy, could not prevail.

But there, in that fishing village, nearly 20 years before, and at a youthful 42, she had that health and stamina. Yet even so, as I've said, several times she very nearly gave up, and just walked out. But what kept her there? We didn't *need* the money for survival.

So let me put it in her own words. "I'd just about quit," she said, "but then I'd look at those other women, most older than I, and some much older than I. Day after day they were still there. I just couldn't walk out on them."

There was no union, and no "sweatshop" either; no slavery, no Simon Legree, only a challenge. In the midst of that droning machinery, standing those long hours there with that never ending stream of fish coming along, one *could* believe that this would last forever; and a heart could fail, knowing that the body could *not* last forever.

But the mind can rule our emotions, if we will it to, and the mind reminded, "This is the harvest; this will be all over in eight or ten weeks." And so they were lifted and inspired, even before the end, with that sense of victory, of elation, of accomplishment: "We did it, we did it."

One day, during a long break when some machinery had failed, she had a long talk with a co-worker friend who was much older than she.

"Mary," she inquired, "What are you doing here in this grueling, cold, wet slime line?"

And the wise, wise, perceptive answer, "Well, in Seattle I can survive on my very small income, but I'd have to live in a shack to do so, and so be looked down on as that poor, little old lady. But here, I can live in a shack, and be fully accepted.

"But more," she continued, "I can work the short canning season here and be part of the Spirit of Harvest that grips the town as the fish come in. And when the season ends, I can feel with all the rest that exhilarating sense of victory, of elation, of accomplishment, 'We did it; we did it.' That is why I live in Cordova, instead of Seattle, or even Arizona."

Margaret Anderson

Without wanting to get involved with philosophy or psychology, I will say that I have found, over the years, and know that most women will agree, that women are more *apt* to develop a "pecking order" than men do. Certainly that was very evident among the slime line crew.

On her first break, Alma was, for some reason, one of the first to walk into the lunch room and sit down. One of the other women quickly warned her, "You'd better not sit there; Margaret won't like it." So she moved to the foot of the table. Margaret was, I believe, Bobbie Anderson's aunt, and so part Indian. She was tall, serious, highly skilled at her work, strong, and strong willed. Although I don't think she had any official supervisory capacity, she "ruled the roost" there. No one challenged her, and Alma had no reason to, so she just stayed out of the way.

Alma herself was physically beautiful, but small, quiet, reserved, very ladylike before the world. She did not go looking for trouble. However, as we shall later see, she *was* her feisty, French Canadian mother's daughter. She had some flaws, some serious ones; and she made some mistakes, some serious mistakes. But cowardice, or any expression of cowardice was *not* one of either.

Probably two or three weeks into the job, these two, part-Indian women clashed. Right in front of Alma's position, was a gate that, open, allowed fish that had not yet been trimmed, to go on down to the last two positions, and closed, deflected those untrimmed fish to a return belt, so that they could go around again. Alma was to watch, out of the corner of her eye, of course, how the women on down the line were doing, and so open or close that gate as needed.

Apparently, Margaret got to believing that Alma was not doing it right and started shouting down the line, "Close that gate; open that gate; close that gate." After a few hours of that, it was clear to Alma that this was harassment, *not* instruction; and she got her belly full. That fighting spirit she had inherited from that French Canadian mother boiled over. She stabbed that big knife into that block, and walked around behind the other women and up to Margaret Anderson. And then she told her, in waterfront language she was surprised to know she knew, to back off.

When she walked back to the position, she was chilled to find that knife so deeply stabbed into that wooden block, that she had to bend it back and forth several times to break it free. What if, in her fury, she had taken the knife with her?

For a moment, she just stood there, her heart pounding. And then she looked up, and across the room where a Filipino friend was tending that Iron

Chink. No words could exchange, of course, above the roar of machinery, but that almost impassive face held just the hint of a smile. And then one eye gave a subtle wink, and his head a subtle but telling nod of approval. She felt better and drove back into her work.

But remember that pecking order? At the very next break, I don't think Margaret came into the lunch room. But as Alma did, two women told her, "Sit here, Alma." She was no longer the baby chick in the flock. It was a hard way to earn her wings but those had been the Cordova Cannery slime line crew's unwritten rules. Although driven to it, she had fought by those rules, and won her position there.

I don't think that she and Margaret ever became friends; and as always, I think that is a loss. Margaret Anderson was a capable, skilled, highly respected member of the Cordova Community, but like us all, she needed friends. I know that Alma would very much liked to have really been her friend.

CHAPTER 12

Prince William Sound, Alaska

[All over Prince William Sound, up the vast fiords, and into tiny coves, one is struck with the impossible, yet insistent fact that you are cruising at sea level among the mountaintops. This joining of two extremes, each powerfully impressive in itself, brought forth this poem, written, or more correctly, discovered, at sea under a brilliant northern sun:]

> Out in the middle of a Switzerland sea
> I gaze at the mountains, and then look at me.
> There's an ocean around me that drops off and away
> as the curve of this globe commands it to stay
> in the arc that was ordered when molten earth formed
> and clouds of the ether thundered and stormed...

From my book, *ISLANDS OF EXPERIENCE*.

These words, and the few verses that followed, very literally burst in a flood from my heart and pen on an early August day as I headed for home after policing the last salmon harvest in this area. It had been a glorious morning. The sparkling, silver sea, its curving arc, rarely seen so clearly, the splendor of new, unworn mountains jeweling the boundaries of that sea, all immersed me so deeply in the power of their presence that there was no holding back that flood of words.

No, I shall not be so audacious as to write a chapter, in one small book, and try to paint a complete word picture of this so unique region on this earth. Oh yes, there are the fiords of Norway, the ragged teeth of the coasts of Maine, the "Cote Sauvage," the savage western coast of France. But we were there, in Prince William Sound, and my heart, and mind, and pen must carry at least a few others into some of that experience.

So let me leap ahead a few weeks and borrow words from my Journal; and then we shall return to the story.

Monday, July 5, 1965: "Up at 1:30 A.M., and pulled out with my skiff into a beautiful, partly cloudy, pre-dawn to patrol Unakwik Inlet and Miners Bay. The bay is close to Meares Glacier, and what a fantastic wonderland that bay was, with its purple, benched cliffs looking like huge replicas of the sacrificial pyramids of Mazatlan, and with waterfalls slashing those cliffs like streaks of white lightning. What an experience to be cruising at sea level among the mountain tops, weaving between ten thousand icebergs from 50 lbs to 500 tons,—sliding close to islands that seemed to be standing on tiptoes from the bottom of the sea, and here and there a patch of low, lazy and lacy mist gracing the entrance to a hidden cove, and all unspoiled, and all mine."

Stepping from the Copper Sands into Prince William Sound was like stepping through the veil of a fourth dimension. One could almost wonder if even we were the same beings. There on the sands, the glory and the terror was the very shallowness of the waters, and the low, nearly sea level flatness of the sands. There, the yielding, yet unyielding sand turned the easy, rolling swells of the ocean into the liquid teeth of breakers that slashed and tore at any who would dare to embrace her beauty. Yet once into her arms, the protected coves gave peace and comfort and rest.

That same peace was not to be found on Prince William Sound. Splendor, glory, severe beauty, yes; and there was a call to come to her, and to come back again. But that call was a siren call, for Prince William Sound could destroy, and do so treacherously, especially in winter. More than one small ship, and with an experienced Captain in command, has run from the storm and found refuge in a cove sheltered from the hounding sea. And then, in the dark of the night, they have found themselves fighting for their lives against the mountain winds, screaming down through those gashes in the towering stone in gales of 100 mph and more.

I do not know the record speed of those winds, but I am certain that they have been recorded in excess of 120 mph. And, there is a reason. We innocently think of air as a weightless gas, if we think of it at all. But air has great weight, and cold air is *much* heavier than warm air. As the winter air over interior Alaska gets colder, and heavier, and the air over the waters of Prince William Sound and the Gulf of Alaska that carry the warm Japanese Current, stayed warmed by that water, a tremendous pressure gradient develops.

The tall, stone walls of the coastal mountains block the flow from the high pressure to the low—except, as I've said, where it can scream through, through those gashes in that towering stone.

And it takes no geologist to see how those gashes were made. Birthplace of earthquakes, Prince William Sound is obviously also the birthplace of mountains and fiords, as the slowly drifting crust of this earth has, over a relatively few centuries, literally torn the stone apart, leaving holes out in the middle of that inland sea as much as half a mile deep. The epicenter of the great 1964 Alaskan Earthquake was, I believe, near Port Wells, or College Fiord.

A brief study of the chart of Prince William Sound, and one can, in the mind's eye, push most of those islands, and fiord walls back together, and see them fit perfectly. And the area is so geographically young, there are almost no beaches. That gives the rugged shores the sharp beauty of youth, but the brashness of youth prevails.

And there really is no autumn in Prince William Sound. When the fall equinox comes, and summer ends on September 21st, Winter comes in like a slamming door. For a couple of years, I was the Marine Traffic Agent in charge of the Anchorage Office of the Alaska Marine Highway System. One of our ships, the little *Chilkat*, besides serving Cordova from Valdez, also carried summer tourists between Valdez and Whittier, between about May 1 and Sept. 30. I pleaded with the Juneau authorities to end the season no later than Sept. 15 because 90 percent of

> **UNITED STATES COAST GUARD**
> SERIAL NUMBER 77027
> L-214
>
> **CERTIFICATE OF REGISTRY**
> **TO U.S. MERCHANT MARINE STAFF OFFICER**
>
> This is to certify that **DEAN ROBERT NICHOLS** having given satisfactory evidence that he is qualified to serve as a staff officer on vessels of the U.S. Merchant Marine in the grade of **PURSER** has, by direction of the Commandant of the Coast Guard, been registered as such staff officer in accordance with the Act of August 4, 1939, and the regulations issued thereunder.
>
> Given under my hand this **TENTH** day of **JUNE** 19**75** at port of **ANCHORAGE, ALASKA**
>
> H. W. COHOON, LT., USCG
> Officer in Charge, Marine Inspection
> By direction

r a few years, in Anchorage, Alaska, Capt. Dean was the Marine Traffic ent for the Alaska Marine Highway System. This qualified him for the k of "Purser," so he applied for the license. It is not limited to five years for each issue, so never needs renewing, as do the other two.

our dock damage, from that ship being slammed about by suddenly appearing winter winds, occurred during those last 15 days. (I did not succeed, of course. "Daddy" always knows best.) But winter is cruel, unforgiving, merciless on Prince William Sound.

But those summers... Like a giant cat, that *can* rip out one's life in a few, powerful slashes with her claws, Prince William Sound purrs gently, under the summer sun; she is a warm, cuddly feline, even seeming to smile as she shares her sensuous, youthful beauty.

F. M. J., Wednesday, June 16, 1965: "Slept in, for a change, and finally over to the Office just before noon. Checked with Bob and found I have a load of four stakeout men, and a mountain of supplies for Coghill, and our cabin base at Eshamy, early Friday morning."

A few years before, we had taken a Pilot for KLM, Royal Dutch Airlines, and a Dutch Stewardess, the 80 miles or so by road north of Anchorage, and then 10 miles in our fast runabout across the lakes and channels to our cabin in the wilderness. We spent a lovely day, letting that peaceful wilderness wash the world away. Those most interesting and stimulating people, who have travelled the world, told us often, "But there is no place in all the world like Alaska." As we were racing back down that Alaskan pond, Renee said, almost with wonder, "What an experience." And so:

F. M. J., Friday, June 18, 1965: "Left Cordova at 7:00 A.M., with stakeouts, Tom Cates, and Ross Clements, and Phil Crase, and Ray Vroble, and 2500 lbs of food and gear aboard. A real load... Dropped Tom and Ross, and 600 lbs off at unbelievably deep, secluded and beautiful, Billy's Hole on Long Bay. Talk about a 'Hurricane Hole.' *No* storm could reach a boat there. It was almost round, and just enough room to swing freely all points on our anchor. As we entered, our fathometer was reading 180 feet, then leaped to 20 feet, and back to over 100 feet. And then on entering that 100 foot or so, natural stone walled canal into that inner lagoon, we found the channel deeper than it was wide.

"And then a five hour or so run on to strikingly beautiful Eshamy Lagoon. Ferried our two men, and some of the remaining ton of gear ashore and up to the cabin... Anchored for the night in a lovely, tiny, protected cove, off a clean, gravel beach at the east end of the Lagoon, about 11:00 P.M., and listened to a radio station in Anchorage... On the way through the icebergs off Columbia Glacier, we chipped off some 10 lb chunks of that clear, hard ice to cool our fruit and vegetables... It was almost flat calm all day, except for the last two-hour run on in. But now we are at anchor in the deep, penetrating silence and stillness of the lagoon... It has been a long, 16-hour day, but, as Renee would say, 'What an experience.'"

F. M. J., Saturday, June 19, 1965: "Radio said there were winds forcast to 50 knots out on the Sound, so we lay all day in Eshamy, and worked on my boat, and brought my paperwork up to date, while the boys unloaded the rest of the gear, and set up the cabin... Rain all day, but still and beautiful in this 'Mountain torn' lagoon..."

F. M. J., Sunday, June 20, 1965: "The Marine Forcast wouldn't come through on my radio, but I finally got Yakutat Radio on 3230, and they called FAA for me, and relayed the Marine Forcast—Winds SW, 5 to 15. So I weighed anchor about 9:30, and headed home...

"A beautiful, mostly clear day, with only the long, 6 to 8 foot ground swells rolling in from the Pacific through Hinchinbrook Entrance. I held 80 degrees on the compass for 5 hours, from Eleanor Island to Gravina Point, for 40 some miles, right across the middle of that Switzerland Sea... Raining, naturally, when we arrived in Cordova about 7:00 P.M...

"There was a beautiful Father's Day card here from my son, Lloyd, with a short, but warm personal note. I had written *him* a letter today, out in the middle of that Sound, that incredible Prince William Sound... It is good to have a son."

CHAPTER 13

Problems; the Sands; and History

We took a couple of needed days off, and then:

F. M. J. Wednesday, June 23, 1965: "Put a new fuel pump on today. The engine is still cutting out as if starving for gas at higher speeds, so I called in two mechanics; but neither could find the trouble. It does run OK up to 2500 rpms, so decided to sail tomorrow anyway. But I'm kind of discouraged tonight."

I know that I said, a chapter or two back, that after we cleared up the oil problem that that Chevrolet ran, true to its heritage. Well, after a few more problems, it did. It wasn't that Chevrolet's fault that it was born a gasoline engine, and then placed in a wet, wet environment for which all that sensitive, electrical ignition system was not designed.

And I am not really sure that all the above is really part of a romantic story of the sea, here, in this dramatically unique place. But maybe the next, short excerpt from my Journal will convey just a bit of the drama that that less than perfectly healthy engine provided.

F. M. J. June 24, 1965: "Gathered gear for the Test Fish Crew, shopped for groceries, and loaded my boat. To the Standard Oil Dock to fuel up, and to load three barrels of gas and two of stove oil for the cabin skiffs.

"Left Cordova on the tide at 1:30 P.M., and across the flats and picked up Bob Barone off Eyak. We had been told that, with this high a tide, we could probably get on over to Walhalla inside the bars. We wallowed around in the sand for an hour, and then discarded that 'brilliant idea,' and headed for sea out the Egg Island Entrance, and back through the surf, just before dark, to Walhalla.

"The engine is still cutting out above 2500 rpms, which made it a bit disconcerting, crossing the bars."

F. M. J. Friday, June 25, 1965: "Up at 5:30, and ran to the Walhalla gas cache, before the tide was too high, so that we could see the banks. There we unloaded two barrels of gas.

"Bob asked, 'How are we going to get those heavy barrels off this boat and up on the shore?'

"Actually, I didn't know, but I just said, 'Oh, we'll make it somehow.'

"Earlier, by some curious inspiration, I had thrown a 12 to 14 foot, rough, 2 X 6 plank aboard. When we reached nearly the end of that narrow slough, and with the safety of a rising tide, we laid the *Brant*'s side snug against that steep, sandy bank, holding her there with a pair of anchors set in the soft soil of the land. Then we set that 2 X 6 from the gunwale, over to the shore. Together, we tipped those 300 lb barrels up onto the gunwale, rolled them, balancing carefully, to that 2 X 6, and on over to the shore. The hardest part of the job was rolling them another 50 feet up through the soft sand to the cache. But we were finished in 20 or 30 minutes.

"Bob was impressed, and said so. Secretly, I was impressed myself at how easily it had been done."

But now, a quarter of a century later, I realize that I had just acted upon the example teaching of a most resourceful father. When asked, "How are we going to do that, Dad?" he would answer, "I don't know yet, but we're going to do it." And we did.

Returning to my Journal for this day: "As I started up to run back out to the main anchorage for breakfast, the engine started and ran OK, but all my accessories were dead—no lights, no instruments, no radio.

"Later, Barone took the skiff to run after the Test Fish Crew. So I started in on the wiring. All of the contacts on the main electrical panel came off, were polished and soundly reconnected; a new ground wire was installed; but still no power. So I took all five batteries out, cleaned up all the terminals, some of which were very badly corroded, and put it all back together. Everything worked.

"The crew came back and picked up their oil and gas, and finally we had our supper about 8:00 P.M. Then Barone and I argued religion, politics, and economics till midnight."

Reference that electrical system. Obviously, that was not that Chevrolet's fault, or even a gasoline engine's fault. The previous Captain had neglected his maintenance. Salt water, dripping off boots and oilskins, had dripped on down through a joint in the cabin sole and onto the terminals. So later, I just built a plastic cover over those batteries. But the electrical systems of any ship at sea are vulnerable to the salt that even drifts with that heavy, moisture laden air. That equipment, like human relationships, needs never ending, tender loving care if we expect them to return fidelity to us in their turn.

And the Good Book says, "All things are held together by His power." And though some speak of animate and inanimate objects, I had felt, since childhood, that always, if I cared well for a piece of equipment, especially one which very literally carried my life, then, when the storms raged, when the margins were no more, that I had a right to expect faithful service in return. Near the end of this book, that contract is graphically portrayed.

But reference Bob Barone: He was different. I wouldn't say he was effeminate; he was a healthy, strong, very male young man; also from New York, I believe. But he just would not use the four letter words, or even some three letter or five letter words, that most other young men used to "more precisely express themselves."

I remember one time when three of us were sitting in a Fish and Game pickup on the main street in Cordova. A young woman, well endowed, and obviously proud of it, came down the board sidewalk. And Bob remarked, in his very proper way, "My goodness, that young lady has the most well-developed pair of mammary glands I do believe I've ever seen."

We understood what he was saying. Oh, he was a male animal alright; and, he did his job, and well.

F. M. J. Saturday, June 26, 1965: "We were up early to listen to the Marine Forcast on the *Brant*'s excellent radio. It sounded good, so we had our breakfast, and weighed anchor about 8:30.

"Although not really stormy, it was a choppy, uncomfortable ride all the way to Strawberry entrance. The steepening Pacific swells were hitting us square on our port beam. But 5 hours after having our breakfast aboard that workboat of the fishing fleet, in that 'far-away-place-with-the-strange-sounding-name,' we were home. It is always good to be home."

F. M. J. Sunday June 27, 1965: "A day off; but a different day. We touched a bit of history this day. Or maybe it would be better said, history touched us.

"We packed a picnic lunch, and drove east, past the airport a few miles, to Sheridan Glacier, and walked on that ancient ice, now slowly melting, and returning to the sea from whence it came. How long ago had the snowflakes fallen that, finally reaching that critical 100 feet or more, had pressed themselves into that hard, clear mineral that is glacier ice?

"We drove on to mile 27, and walked across the fatally damaged 'million dollar bridge,' and on across Round Island to the completely fallen span. What a beautiful trip it has been, and so loaded with that spirit of history, that we felt, and shared a deep and genuine sadness with the crying waters, swirling around those broken piers, and the fallen, rusting steel."

For more detailed history, and for a dramatic, true story, read *THE IRON TRAIL*, by Rex Beach, the building of the Copper River Railroad. For a bridge to cost over one million dollars 80-some years ago meant that heroic effort had to have been made to bring that railroad into existence.

And it had long been the dream of those with vision to build, finally, a highway link between Cordova and the rest of the world, up that old rail bed, using those still sound and intact railroad bridges.

But fate was not to allow Cordova that ending of her isolation. The massive, Alaskan earthquake on March 27, 1964, did in five minutes what years of Winter storms and Spring floods could not do, and left those magnificent evidences of man's genius and determination lying in the swirling waters of the Copper River, and being scoured by her copper sands.

We were indeed, touched by history, that day. And even these many years later, as I write these lines, I poignantly feel the sadness of that day. It stabs one to the heart to see dreams die. Let us quickly "return to the waters."

CHAPTER 14

We Voyage West Again

Ashore Long Enough

F. M. J. Monday June 28, 1965: "...Worked on the *Brant* most of the day. This afternoon, cleaned up the bilge and checked out all the fuel lines and suction standpipe. All was clear, and gas will even siphon at 45 gallons per hour to the fuel pump...

"We were invited over to Bob and Kathy Anderson's this evening. Bob had brought in 50 lbs of butter clams. Charlie Allen came in, and we all stuffed ourselves with hot clams, right out of the shell, and dipped in butter. That bountiful sea keeps giving."

F. M. J. Wednesday, June 30, 1965: "Our last day in that miserable 'lovely little trailer house.'

"Raining hard all night, and drizzle all day... Hauled a load of 'things' up to the shack this morning. ...Storm picking up, so I walked down to the harbor, and warmed up the engine, and checked for an oil leak, and brought my paperwork up to date.

"Bob came down, and State Fish & Game Board Member, Dick Jansen, and his wife came over, and the four of us huddled by the oil stove in that tiny cabin, drinking tea, and watching the storm, and talking fishing regulations for a couple hours."

(A certain amount of politicking *is* part of the job, you know; and as I remember, Dick Jansen was a good man. He knew the sea, and fishing, and he was intelligent enough to apply that knowledge in the political arena. But I cannot pass this moment without remembering again the ambivalence of a quiet, peaceful exhilaration, that special joy of the sea, as the four of us sat so close, talking in that warm, snug cabin, watching the storm, and feeling, now and then, the tug of the boat against her lines. "The bosom of the sea:" how poetic, yet how poignantly true.)

Continuing from my Journal: "My wife had all our things moved up to the shack by this evening. Our new home is really very comfortable. We bought a jug to celebrate... We decided that this was, after all, no shack. It is a comfortable, cozy cabin; and the view of the harbor, Orca Inlet, and the islands is magnificent."

F. M. J. Friday, July 2, 1965: "Finished installing a new, electric fuel pump on the engine. It still cut out at over 2000 rpms at the dock. So I installed a new set of sparkplugs. It seemed to run better at the dock, so I took her out for a run, and the engine nearly died at 1800. I returned to the dock and called Juneau.

A $65 a month "Cabin," and a million dollar view. Cordova Boat Harbor, and misty Orca Inlet. July 1, 1965.

"Ted Bachman was on vacation, so I talked to the Vessels Supervisor, Ed Nielsen, who, in effect, said we'd have to work it out here.

"I think he said it out of irritation, but it was sound advice. I had to, and did, start to think. I remembered an old mechanic of years before, who had told me, 'Ninety percent or more of all problems with a gasoline engine are electrical.' So I checked the ignition again, and decided to try a new condenser...

"Still raining. Tonight, I moved the *Brant* over to our new, and permanent, Fish and Game dock, since, finally, they have a ramp down. It is so much better now; even our small ships seem to feel better, nestled in their own berths."

Finally, the M/V *Brant*, securd to her very own float.
My tough, little skiff secured alongside.
Cordova Boat Harbor. July 2, 1965.

F. M. J. Saturday, July 3, 1965: "...Unable to get a regulation condenser, in this fishing village, so bought one 'for a V-8, 12V,' put it on, and took the *Brant* out for a test run. That engine was a Chevrolet again. I almost felt ashamed of myself for being so slow to help her. Even a Chevrolet, if neglected long enough, will complain... Fueled up at the oil dock; and shopped for groceries for another voyage, and then met with Bob, and two 'Stakeouts,' and Cabin Skiff operators for a briefing... We have been ashore long enough; the sea is calling again."

Somewhere Among The Crags

F. M. J. Sunday, July 4, 1965: "...Out early and up to the cafe to hustle out my crew, Jerry Baron, and two Stakeouts, Tom Wright and Dick Smeltzer, and get them aboard. We finally cleared the harbor just after 8:00, that engine purring like a contented cat, but one happily on the prowl. We had Jerry's cabin skiff, *Wahoo*, in tow."

It was a beautiful, calm, though cloudy day, as we cruised easily the few miles NE, up Orca Inlet, around Salmo Point, and then back, WSW, down Orca Bay, for an hour, past Simpson Bay, and Sheep Bay, and then west for another hour or so. With the long, low, almost imperceptible ground swells from the ocean, through Hinchinbrook Entrance, lifting our hull and her cargo, we cruised on past Port Gravina (really a deep, green fiord,) then WNW for yet another hour or so past Knowles Head and on out

Cruising among the mountains on the channeled sea.
Prince William Sound. July, 1965.

across the northern part of this quiet, inland sea to just south of Fairmount Island.

There, we installed Jerry's compass and taught him how to use it, and checked him out on his new radio.

"But I've never talked on a radio before in my life," he protested again.

"Oh, OK," we said, "Here is the on button, this is your volume control, your frequency selector, your squelch control, and here on your mike is your 'Press to talk' button, OK?"

It wasn't really OK; we could see that on his face. But as I said before, this was a very capable young man. Mixed with his trepidation, I could see the rising in his spirit to a challenge. So we shoved him off a hundred yards or so, and ran through a few practice radio calls, and told him to head for his destination, Coghill.

"You have your charts," I had told him earlier, "It's a glorious day. That's Fairmount Island to the north, and that's Storey Island to the south, the northernmost of the Naked Island Group. Almost due west is Axel Lind Island, and SW of that, about three miles, is The Dutch Group, right there.

"Then go NW between Bald Head Chris Island and the mainland, and stay on a NW course, and it will put you right into Esther Passage. When you come out of Esther Passage, there, turn right up Port Wells, and College Fiord about 10 miles, and you're home at Coghill.

"Oh, by the way, that's about where the epicenter of the 1964 earthquake was."

That sharp young man just shook his head, grinned, and then said, "I'm really not fully convinced, Cap, but if you say I can do it, well, here goes." And he took off.

I felt a little like a Dad, shoving his kid off for his first day of school. But I knew he could do it, and of course, he did.

And then we turned NNW past Olsen Island, and on north up Unakwik Inlet to an unnamed cove to which Bob had directed us. It was some south of Cutthroat Creek, and we could find no name for it on our chart, or in the Coast Pilot, so we named it, "Capt. Nic's Cove."

Like so many coves, in this sea-washed mountain range, it had an island at its mouth, making the cove more of a lagoon. Even though I touched so little of this fingered sea, during that brief summer, I had found so many of these coves, protected at their mouths by an island.

As I have said before, much of the geology of Prince William Sound can be explained by just studying the charts. But even my own imagination could not find a reason for all of those islands at those special spots.

And so we waited for further orders, hidden in a small cove, behind an island, "somewhere among the seawashed crags of Prince William Sound."

CHAPTER 15

The Edges of a Mystery

We quoted, in Chapter 12, an excerpt from my Journal for July 5, I know, but let's quote it again here to keep the flow of the story intact. There will be an additional portion of that day added that tells of a marvelous, yet little known phenomenon.

And so, F. M. J. Monday, July 5, 1965: "Up at 1:30 A.M., and pulled out, alone, with my skiff into a beautiful, partly cloudy, pre-dawn to patrol Unakwik Inlet and Miner's Bay.

"The bay is close to Meares Glacier; and what a fantastic wonderland that bay was, with its purple, benched cliffs, looking like huge replicas of the sacrificial pyramids of Mazatlan, and with waterfalls slashing those cliffs like streaks of white lightning. What an experience, to be cruising at sea level among the mountain tops, weaving between ten thousand icebergs from 50 lbs to 500 tons—sliding close to islands that seemed to be standing on tiptoes from the bottom of the sea, and here and there, a patch of low, lazy, and lacy mist gracing the entrance to a hidden cove, and all unspoiled, and all mine."

My Journal does not record, but my mind remembers vividly, looking north, across that field of scattered ice, and seeing the face of Meares Glacier. I knew my chart; that glacier was not there, could not be there. It was close to 4 miles north to where the inlet turned sharply, east, and then perhaps another half mile around that towering, stone corner to the glacier face. But, there it was, less than three-quarters of a mile away, in crystal clear, graphic detail.

I picked my way toward that "glacier," through those sculptured ice forms, and marveled at the creative beauty. Obviously, the Master Sculptor had been at work, creating this beauty, just for the joy of creating beauty. For had I not been there to see it, in just a few hours, under that northern sun, their shapes would be melted and gone to the sea from whence they came.

But at that moment, it took far less imagination than seeing faces in the clouds, to see horses, and dolphins, and vases, and mermaids, and a hundred other graven images, carved from that hard, clear ice. I moved with reverent awe, alone, among those mute and silent forms that spoke so clearly to my soul.

But as I moved less than half a mile toward that glacier face, it began to break up. And as I moved closer, there were only pieces of it seeming to hang in the trees and rocks on the far shore; and finally it vanished completely. I did not run the few miles on up through that broken ice, but I could see the dark stone at the corner, about 3 miles away.

Most people associate mirages with the desert. Novels, and movies have done that for us. But I have read that there are more mirages in the arctic than on the desert. It is the same principle involved, but actually, the faces between the layers of air of differing temperature are much sharper in the arctic.

In this case, with no wind in the mountains, that cold, cold ice had sent a slow moving, thin layer of very cold air sliding away, and under the much warmer air out over the water. That interface formed, what I believe is termed a refractive mirror, which carried the reflection of that glacier face around the corner, and into my sight.

Continuing from my Journal: "Back to the cove about 5:30, and slept for a few hours.

"Breakfast, and changed oil in the engine, and then, around 2:00 P.M., I took my crew on the same cruise but with the *Brant*. About three miles south of Miners Bay, and stretching clear across the inlet opposite Jonah Bay, was a very narrow, shallow, underwater ridge. I believe it is geologically safe to say that obviously, a short time ago, in geologic time, the face of the glacier had been there, shoving its moraine nearly to the surface.

"With the fathometer on our larger boat now working, and even knowing what the chart was saying, still, it almost made us catch our breaths as we watched that marvelous instrument recording 600 to 700 feet of water, and then in seconds, leaping to less than 15 feet, and then as suddenly, falling away to 600 to 700 feet again.

"As we again came up to Miners Bay, we marveled together at the mystery of the mirage of that 200-foot-high face of a glacier, still standing there, and yet that faded to simple drift ice as we threaded closer, and then reappeared as we moved away."

I don't think the Alaska Dept. of Fish and Game was paying any of us very much money, even for those times. But who could buy an experience such as we had just been given?

F. M. J. Tuesday, July 6, 1965: "We are just waiting, so we all slept late... I whipped up a batch of hotcakes, bacon, and eggs, that tantalizing joy of breakfast, and then the boys took the skiff and went gunkholing... I installed new Fish and Game decals on the *Brant*, and brought my reports and paper work up to date... Beautiful, sunshiny, summer day...

"Bob and Charlie Allen dropped from the sky in the float plane about 9:00 P.M. They want me to deliver my stakeout team to Eaglek Bay. So, after they left, we got itchy, and upped anchor about 10:00 P.M. It was never so dark that I couldn't read my chart, standing out on the afterdeck, although I must admit to a feeling of exciting adventure, feeling and sensing our way, the 12 to 15 miles around and through the islands, and up into the large cove on the east side of Eaglek Bay."

I'd like to interject here, that Dick Smeltzer was another sharp young man, and one with a curiosity. As we cruised down that inlet in the half light of that northern night, he asked, with just a bit of concern, "Have you ever made this trip before?"

And when I answered, "No," he understandably asked, "Then how do you know where you are going?"

So I answered, "A good question, but it's all here on the chart. And even though it is the middle of the night, we can still see large objects a mile or two away. Two miles is about three quarters of an inch on the chart, and at our speed, that's about 15 minutes. We'll just cruise south for half an hour or so and should come up on Olsen Island, right there. Then we'll start curving west for another half hour or so, keeping the mountains off our starboard beam. By then, we should spot those islands, there, off Point Pellew.

"The chart says we have plenty of water between those islands, so we'll turn NNW, and cruise a half mile or so off shore for another ten or fifteen minutes. The fathometer will tell us when we come up on that shallow spot, just at the south edge of our cove."

And that was how it worked out.

It was quite dark, as we turned right, and felt our way NE a little under 2 miles into the large cove, and found another one of those islands, protecting the mouth of the inner lagoon. There, we dropped anchor before the 30-foot wide, 20-foot deep, and 200-yard long entrance to a beautiful, inner lagoon. It was just after midnight.

F. M. J. Wednesday, July 7, 1965: "Tom was asleep, so Smeltzer and I took the skiff and kicker, in the stillness of the deep, midnight dusk, and patrolled the entrance, and then into that inner lagoon. A curious seal, or one resenting our intrusion, kicked up a huge splash, 20 feet from our skiff.

"Back to the *Brant* about 1:30, in the rapidly developing daylight, we rousted Tom out, and ferried all their gear ashore in two, heavy loads. And then, alone, I weighed anchor, just before 3:00 A.M., in the now broad daylight, and headed for home.

"But about 7:00, I realized I had been up for nearly 24 hours, so dropped anchor in the quiet water behind Goose Island, and crashed in my warm bunk for a few hours.

"About 2:00 P.M., I awakened into a magnificent, summer day, fixed a sandwich, and then paddled ashore in my skiff, and explored an abandoned home and boatshop, built at least 50 years ago—a remnant of someone's dreams of riches during the fox farming era on Prince William Sound. Again, the sadness of seeing the sun-bleached skeletons of dreams that have died.

"Finally underway for Cordova about 4:00, and secure at our own berth by 8:00 P.M. It has been a curious voyage, this time. A feeling that we have just touched the edges of the deep mystery that is Prince William Sound, a beckoning mystery that sends, at the same time, a subtle hint of warning.

Would I return, today, if I could? Of course. But I would do so with a deep respect for that warning, and for that mystery.

CHAPTER 16

Odd Stories

I shall always regret that I did not record, or at least make notes of the many dozens of stories, dramatic stories, funny stories, stories of heroism and pathos, victory and defeat, success and failure, that those Cordova Fishermen told. They would make a book of their own.

But let me here tell one I observed, two funny ones told to me, and a couple of others:

Dog Days

Late in the season, after most of the Seattle fishermen had sailed for home, Cordova held what I remember as two "Dog Days."

The word was spread around that, say, Friday and Saturday were the "dog days." If you valued your pet, keep it in or clearly under control for those two days.

And then a small team of men patrolled the town with shotguns or rifles. Any loose dog was shot, and its carcass hauled to the dump.

A vicious, cruel, inhumane treatment of many fine animals? No, I don't think so at all. Dogs multiplied in Cordova. Some breeding there, of course, but mostly, the "outside" boats would bring them as pets, and then, for whatever reason, would sail home without them. That small fishing village could not absorb them all, love them as they might. There was no licensing of dogs in the town, and many people kept the otherwise free-running pets, but once a year, something had to be done.

A surgical operation? Yes, but an effective one, we must agree.

Dog Bite

Proof that real Cordovans loved dogs is the following story:

I don't remember his name, but a true Cordova character was lounging inside the window of the local hardware store. He was idly watching three men, standing in the middle of the main street, talking. (Well, there is not *that* much traffic in Cordova.)

A big, gentle, brown dog walked up behind one of the men and sniffed at his pant leg. The man kicked the dog soundly and sent him off, yelping in pain. The men continued talking.

The "character" eased out of the store, and ambled down the board sidewalk a hundred feet or so, and then back up the street behind the man who had kicked the dog. He signalled to the other two to not notice.

As he slipped up behind the unsuspecting man, he knelt down on the ground, let out a big growl, and grabbed the man on the ankle. The man, certain that he had been bitten, leaped in panic.

But before the man could speak, the character stood up, looked him in the eye, and chastened him with these words: "Don't never kick no dog if he aint doin' you no harm," and he walked away. He had made his point.

Feathers

The ducks and geese were flying, so three friends (yes, they were all three friends, but they were Cordova fishermen too) had been out hunting. They had settled in for the night in a tiny, dirt-floored hut one of the men had out on the delta flats. I believe that one of the men was this same "character."

One of the three had crawled into his down-filled sleeping bag and was blissfully snoring. The "character" and the other man were playing cards or telling yarns. They decided that their snoring friend was too oblivious to the world. So they built a small fire in the middle of the floor, blew out the lamp, and, when the room was well filled with smoke, yelled, "Fire, fire."

The sleeping man awoke in panic, choking on the smoke, and, seeing the flames, came out of that sleeping bag without un-zipping the zipper, feathers exploding through the room.

When he finally saw what had been done to him, and regained some self control, I don't know if he killed the "character" and the other man or not. But it is reported that they nearly died laughing.

Oh how I wish I had recorded more of those stories.

Martin Anderson

The following is most assuredly *not* a biography of this very special, Cordova fisherman. It is rather, just one "snapshot," that I had the opportunity to take in passing.

There even well may be an error or two, as I write about him. But these are the memories his living left with me. Although it is my deepest prayer that someone will, one day soon, research and write a complete biography of him, may I be permitted to share this glimpse of a most unique human being whom God chose to tuck away into this tiny corner of His universe.

Martin seemed to be one of those special few who had the incredible talent to do anything he chose to do, and do it with amazing success. Although he was principally a fisherman, he was noted as, "the best boat builder anywhere around." His "Cordova skiffs," were highly prized, and, I believe, he set a design and construction standard for any others in the area.

With a mind like a computer, and with incredibly skilled hands, guided by that fine mind, he was known to build a 16- to 20-foot, flat bottomed, Cordova skiff in under, I believe, 24 hours, or at most 36. And that was from raw lumber, to painted bottom. And full quality was still there.

I believe he was Bobbie Anderson's uncle, which is why I heard the stories about him.

It is told that he and his fine wife "made and went through several fortunes," even before I met him.

But, that cursed jug.

Martin died a few years later, but my memory of his kind and warm personality tells me that, were he living today, he would just smile, perhaps a bit wistfully, and agree that, yes, it is true, that cursed jug.

In my own nearly 70 years of living, I have known two or three other men like him in that there was such a flow of talent, of intense awareness of life around them, of abundant skills to be exercised, that the very human emotions would simply get overloaded at times. And then the release that the bottle and that camaraderie of the bars gave to them became almost a lifeline to be grasped and held, for but a little while.

No, I am not excusing drunkenness as such. Most is just a lazy escape by those refusing to face ordinary life. But these were special men, loveable men, so incredibly talented men. I don't know how *I* would have done, had *I* to live in that skin, and with that mind.

On the debit side, it was reported that he and his wife, on one period at least, stayed drunk for 6 months or more.

But on the credit side, when the money was all gone, they corked the bottle, sobered up, and went to work, fishing the copper sands.

When I met him at Bobbie's house, the night of the butter clams, he had only a small cabin skiff, but was again successfully fishing, and confidently, and good naturedly building a future again.

And typical of that good nature: I had stated, from a cop's point of view, that I was just a bit curious about so many cabin skiffs painted dark gray.

"It is not that decorative a color," I was saying, "and they are most difficult to see, especially in early morning, before fishing time, and late evening, after closure time."

"Well," Martin was saying, with mock seriousness, "I think you are being unduly suspicious. My skiff is gray, but not because I don't want to be seen."

He was an honest fisherman; I knew that. But I countered with, "I believe you, Martin, but if it was white, it would plainly show that you wouldn't *mind* being seen."

He had to agree; we all laughed, and ate more of those steaming butter clams.

Martin Anderson, a man with a terrible, terrible flaw. Yet in spite of that flaw, as I have said before, he was an incredibly capable, highly respected Cordova fisherman, whom I was privileged to know.

I believe that here is an excellent place to quote again from the Good Book, "Let he who is without sin, cast the first stone."

An Indian Captain

Many of the Indians were indeed excellent fishermen. And I'll say again, certainly there was no evident racial prejudice in Cordova.

In fact, as I was visiting, one day, an obviously very successful husband-wife team aboard their fine, 40-some foot purse seiner, with its attending skiff, and nets, and gear, they mentioned the farm they used to own.

I asked, "What are you doing here?"

They looked at each other and smiled, and told me this story:

"Well, we had grown up on the farm, and loved it and did very well with farming. But one day, we realized that our children were grown, and, we had read, and even dreamed some of Alaska and the fishing life.

"So we decided together, one day, to sell the farm, go to Alaska, buy a boat and become fishermen."

(I was beginning to see why they had been successful farmers, and were now successful fishermen.)

The man continued, "We really knew almost nothing about boats, the sea, and fishing, but, you know, one can learn anything.

"So we asked a lot of questions about boats, and learned the boat we needed. And when we found her, we bought her. Then we asked around some more, and found an Indian fisherman whom we hired as our Captain-teacher for a couple of years. He was an excellent choice, for he not only taught us the mechanics of boating and fishing, but the philosophy and the moral codes of this people as well. And he taught us how to sense, and work with the moods of a sea who will be your friend if you respect her, but who can be a formidable foe if you try to cross her moods.

"We loved the farm; but we must say, *this* is living. And we have to give much credit to our Indian Captain, who now has his own boat, and is still our friend."

I loved these kinds of stories, for they reinforced in me the conviction that there is a fundamental goodness in people, a spontaneous willingness, even an eagerness, to work for their own living, to help, and trust one another, when there is little or no interference from Government.

Oh, I was there, representing Government, the law, and that fact was respected, even appreciated. But I could not, did not even attempt to "Police" them, but rather just remained the focal point of the order they all looked to and desired.

CHAPTER

17

Under The Eye

Bastendorff Beach, the Oregon Coast, April 22, 1989: We; that is, Dusty, my old Shepherd and Golden Lab mix, and I have just returned from a walk beside that incessant sea. And I listened to her soothing song, settling my heart and mind. I felt the gentle push of the wind, tasted the salty mist upon my face, and heard the heavy raindrops tapping their telling message upon my old sou'wester hat before they rolled to the edges and down upon the shoulders of my coat. That warm coat was not waterproof; I was getting wet—and loving it.

For I knew this story was calling again, calling, and more, it was demanding the telling. And there, beside the sea, watching the wet storm, my body, mind, and soul were absorbing, from that rain, and through all five senses, plus a couple more, the very Spirit that makes a story live. I was "there" again, walking the Copper Sands of so long ago.

I think that He Who plans all things, has set me up. And that's OK. There *must* be a Spirit through this story, or it would be a dead thing. I would live—and tell,—among the living.

F. M. J. Cordova, Alaska, July 8, 1965: "Fueled up, shopped for groceries, and loaded a complete 'Stakeout kit' aboard this afternoon. We have a two-man, Stakeout team to deliver to Sawmill Bay, on the west side of Valdez Arm tomorrow.

"...This evening, we dropped over to Don Thornton's, Captain of the State Ferry, *Chilkat*, for a beer and visit. He drew me a detailed chart of Tatitlek Narrows."

F. M. J. Friday, July 9, 1965: "Bob had said, 'Alma has been minding the home port, while you have been putting in some long days, out upon the water. Take her along on this trip as a reward to you both. Besides, I know she is a better cook than any of you.'

"I knew he was right, on all three points.

"So she, Cindy, our loveable Border Collie, and I walked down to the boat about 10:00, stowed the grub, and warmed up the engine.

"Our Stakeout crew, Dennis Roe and Rick Petri, aboard about 11:00, and we were underway moments later under a dry though cloudy sky.

"It rains so much in Cordova because, although it is an ocean port, it is nestled in the heart, or deeply into the edge of the mountains. So our cook was delighted when we cruised out from under the overcast near Goose Island into a glorious, sunny, summer day.

"As said earlier, even before the earthquake, the Tatitlek Narrows demanded 'local knowledge' to safely traverse them. But now, with 6 feet less water, it takes some twisting and turning to clear its rocky shoals. But with Don's 'chart,' we slipped through easily.

"But as we passed under the eye of that Indian fishing village of Tatitlek, we could almost feel the pressure of a dozen pairs of binoculars upon us. And that was OK. The mutual respect between able fishermen and the law had been gently reinforced with our passing.

"But once through the narrows, we met Dezzy Kamerer in our Patrol Cabin Skiff, *Blackfish*, about 6:00 P.M. We followed him up and across Valdez Arm to Sawmill Bay, and transferred our crew, and that always mountain of gear, to Dezzy's skiff. He hauled them deeper into that shallow cove, and put them ashore.

"We ran back across the arm, and up Galena Bay, and dropped anchor in the soft, underwater delta ground of Indian Creek. Dezzy joined us there later for an excellent steak dinner.

"Later, in the early dusk, we took a dipnet over to the creek and caught a couple Chum, or Dog salmon for tomorrow's dinner."

Now again, before any reader gets "righteously indignant," please remember that this was over 29 years ago, we were wasting nothing; and besides, doesn't the Good Book say, "Do not muzzle the ox that is treading out the grain."? No, of course one could not do such today. But *then*, it was part of the adventure of this story. I apologize not at all.

F. M. J. Saturday, July 10, 1965: "We were awake at 7:00; and it was so still and beautiful, we had to get out into the warm, morning sun. Such rich, green, purple, white, and towering mountains leaping skyward from the edges of the sea...

"We had Dezzy over for breakfast, and then, in my skiff, he took us on a patrol, deeper into the bay, weaving between a number of small islands, and through a narrow, stone-edged channel into a nearly land-locked lagoon, named, appropriately, 'The Lagoon.' What a startlingly beautiful place. Again, something He must have made, just for the joy of creating beauty.

"Back to our little ship, we had that salmon dinner. The Chum, or Dog salmon is much less prized than the Sockeye, Chinook, or even Silver; but we were most pleasantly surprised at the delightful, though delicate flavor. The meat was nearly as white as halibut, though not with that special flavor, and would not be recognized as salmon at all. But we had a real, seafood dinner, fresh from that ever-giving sea.

"We weighed anchor about 1:30, with the *Blackfish* in tow. Back through the Narrows, back under the eye of that Indian village, we dropped Dezzy off off Port Fidalgo, and cruised on home to Cordova by 9:30... We had slipped under the clouds again, off Port Gravina, although no rain or wind."

Most of our Stakeout Crews did their jobs honestly, and well. But we did have one who couldn't resist the temptation. So they rowed out to the first Purse Seiner that came into the bay, and offered, for a price of course, to look the other way while they ran a few sets inside the markers. Fortunately (at least for the law) they had contacted an honest fisherman, who not only said no, but who reported the incident to Bobbie Anderson. We sent the boys home.

CHAPTER
18

A Fantastic Way to Make a Living

For the next ten or twelve days, we lay in the harbor, like a contented sea lion, basking on the unmoving shore, and resting from a long swim in the ever-moving sea. I slept in my own bed at night, and ate a woman's cooking, as only a lonely sailor can appreciate.

And we spent a few days, catching up on some overdue maintenance on my little ship. Water is so gentle; why, one can move it with a little finger and not notice the effort.

Still, there is a cumulative strength in the waters, and any boat that will move upon them must work, hard work. And now and then she needs special attention, help and care to bring her back to full health. We gave her that care.

But there were a couple of incidents, during that time, that yet tell more of the story.

F. M. J., Wednesday, July 14, 1965: "Today I washed down the *Brant*, hull and house, outside. One full day of hard work; but she looks beautiful...

"... Art Gunderson installed a new oil stove in our shack today. It has a water heater attached. What luxury, real, running hot water."

As I've said, the *Brant* was fiberglass, white, with black trim, which certainly gave her a snappy, Police Boat look. But boats slowly get dirty.

So one sunny day, I tried some Boraxo and warm water on that fiberglass, and, using a big sponge, worked on a couple of dirty spots on the sides of the wheelhouse. The combination worked amazingly well; and the result was startling. A new boat emerged. So I went on to wash the entire house.

I was younger then, of course, but 4 hours later I was so pleased, and proud of the result, that I started in on the hull. That took another 4 hours; but again, the result was phenomenal. Like a beautiful, young woman, dressed for a ball, I know she beamed at the knowledge of what her beauty was saying to others.

At the time, I was totally unaware that anyone else had noticed my work; and I really didn't care. But a few days later, a salty old fisherman walking by said, "That was some 'soogee job' you did on that boat the other day."

I appreciated the genuine compliment, but it reminded me again that my entire comportment there, among those quietly independent people, was observed in great detail. Without at all knowing at the time, I had woven yet another thread into the fabric of our mutual respect and trust.

F. M. J., Thursday, July 15, 1965: "Cloudy to partly cloudy all day, but no rain; and it was hot. It must have been over 60 degrees..."

Today, we live near Roseburg, Oregon, where, in late summer, the thermometer occasionally registers over 100 degrees. I have determined that my own maximum temperature is 94 degrees. Above that it is "hot," and it hurts. One has a "right" to complain, "It surely is hot." But there, beside the cool sea, it was "hot" at 60 degrees.

What significance has all that to this story? I don't know. But it's kind of interesting, isn't it?

F. M. J., Thursday, July 22, 1965: "We sail again tomorrow, so fueled up the Brant this morning... Bob at the house for coffee when we saw the *Shad* come in with a team from the Sport Fish Division. So we walked down and transferred their gear over to the *Brant*..."

I was to learn much, over the next few weeks, of the differences in point of view of the fishery, between the Commercial Fishery and the Sport Fishery. Some of those differences, as with most differences, were merely prejudicial, of course. But there were very real, and understandable, differences that needed to be worked out in fair compromise. But cruising with these men was a new, and thus most interesting experience.

F. M. J., Friday, July 23, 1965: "Down to my boat by 7:00, and took my two passengers for this trip aboard, and cleared the harbor moments later. Biologist, Ed Jones, and assistant, Lynn Nutter were both outgoing men, and good conversationalists.

"There was light, intermittent rain all day, but no wind; so, after we made Salmo Point, we had an easy, pleasant cruise WSW for 25 miles or so, off Hawkins Island, to Johnstone Point on

Hinchinbrook Island, and then another 12 or so miles SW to Bear Cape and around into Port Etches, and anchored in Constantine Harbor.

"We were cruising an easy 8 knots or so; and 40 miles is 5 hours, so it was time for lunch together. And then the boys left with the skiff to survey a stream, and I paddled back out into Port Etches to watch two Purse Seiners make a couple sets each, and then checked their licenses. They were strong, but kind and gentle men, especially the Captains.

(There are mean men, on the sea, but not very many. I think they just do not survive. The sea demands patience, and that makes for strength, and character, and gentleness, the triple marks of a real man.)

Continuing from my Journal: "Back to our anchorage just inside the entrance to Constantine Harbor, and picked up Jones and Nutter. We had a terrific steak supper... The small Purse Seiner, *Frustration*, with Skipper Bob Blake and his brother Pete, stopped in for a two-hour visit."

I believe this was the boat that I had hailed and asked if I could check licenses. The Captain called back, "This is our last set, can we finish first?"

So I called back, "Sure, I'll be anchored up just inside the entrance. Stop by before you anchor up for the night."

Later, after they had pulled alongside, and we had introduced ourselves, Bob said, "You know, Officer, I really appreciate what you did out there."

"Well," I answered, "I'm really here *for* you; to protect *your* livelihood. If you don't make a profit, none of us have a job."

I absolutely could not have survived as an effective Protection Officer without the cooperation of the honest fishermen, that 90 percent very real men and women.

But back to that steak supper. Again I was blessed to have a good and willing cook aboard in Ed Jones. I did have a small problem with Nutter. He wanted to do his part; he was a real worker, and felt guilty, enjoying superb meals, and doing nothing. "Let me clean up," he insisted.

But, though I was a Protection Officer for the Alaska Department of Fish and Game, Captain of one of their Patrol Boats, in my galley, I was a fussy, little old lady.

"No offense, Lynn, really," I insisted. "I do appreciate your willingness. But it really is easier for me to clean up, and put things away where I am used to them. You just relax and let your boss, and your Captain, serve you." He was a fine young man.

This story is not meant to be a travelog of the geology of Prince William Sound, but I must say something about that natural jetty that made Constantine Harbor that perfectly protected water that it was.

I did take a course in Geology in Alaska, so *of course* that makes me a Geologist. But I also have watched the moving of the large, gravel stones that finally made the over three mile long Homer Spit in Kachemak Bay at the SW end of the Kenai Peninsula. And here was the same, natural phenomenon in action.

About a mile south of the NW side of Port Etches lies Phipps Island. The NW outer corner of Port Etches, is Bear Cape, a high, cliff of stone. The angle at which the incessant swells from the Pacific Ocean strike Bear Cape, means that, as the rocks are now and then broken off and rolled around, and made into gravel, they are also slowly worked to the right, or SE toward the outer end of Phipps Island. Today, there is almost a perfect jetty, a bit over a mile long, 20 or more feet above the sea, and maybe 150 to 250 feet wide, and reaching all the way from Bear Cape to the outer end of Phipps Island. On the outside are the waves of the Pacific Ocean; on the inside, the calm, still waters of Constantine Harbor.

Dare I conjecture at how long it took to build that jetty? Well, I don't know if Geologists themselves really know. But in my brief observation of the moving stones there, and along the shore north of Homer Spit, I would have to say that, geologically speaking, it took a very short time, perhaps less than a few hundred years.

Yes, you can move water with your little finger, and hardly notice the effort. But when the molecules of that gentle fluid work together, with the soft, silky threads of the woven wind, even the stones will not long remain.

F. M. J., Saturday, July 24, 1965: "Today, Capt. Rudy Becker and I had a pretty firm confrontation. Although we later became good friends, this day, his remark, 'That just might make a man angry, you know,' had a real edge to it. I couldn't really blame him, but, the law is the law; I had my job to do."

I had watched them seining for awhile with my glasses, and saw a young boy helping. That was not unlawful, if the boy was licensed; but if children are not, they must not touch the gear. It was a mistake sometimes made. So when they finished a set, I swung alongside and checked licenses. There was none for the boy.

"It should be at the Parks Cannery," Rudy insisted, "They were slow issuing it; and we had to sail."

"But it *is* supposed to be aboard, Captain," I insisted, "But if we can contact Cordova, and confirm that the license is there, well, we can waive writing you up. But if we can't confirm it, I'll *have* to write you up; you know that."

And that was when that rugged fisherman's face darkened, and he said, "That could make a man angry, you know."

My little radio wouldn't reach Cordova over the island mountains, but we found a large tender, with a much larger radio, and they made contact with the Parks Cannery in Cordova. "Yes, the Becker boy's license is here in my hands," was the reassuring reply.

So I waived the charges. Rudy knew, and respected the law. He was one of the 90 percent. I could see that.

Continuing from my Journal: "We spent the rest of the day, ferrying my Sport Fish team all over Port Etches, checking the surprising number of streams, and small lakes there.

"Anchored for the night back just inside the entrance to Constantine Harbor."

I had gone with them on a couple surveys, and learned a lesson in fish biology. Biologists say that salmon develop an amazing capacity to live out of water for longer periods than normal when they are driving up streams to spawn. We have watched them valiantly "swim" for 50 yards across not much more than wet gravel before they found enough water depth to at least get their mouths under the water surface.

And such is the powerful, primal urge to complete the mating call that I have watched, from only a few feet away, an old, scarred and torn, nearly white male, one eye gone from some bird's attack, gamely defend "his" female against a younger male. Survival of the fittest there, before my eyes.

F. M. J., Sunday, July 25, 1965: "We couldn't sleep past 6:00 A.M., so we had our breakfast, and steaming coffee, and out into an incredibly beautiful, warm, summer day, here, on this northern, inland sea.

"We checked a few more streams inside Port Etches, and then ran out to anchor off that amazing gravel dike. The skiff ashore, and I walked the beach, and even lay on the warm gravel while the boys checked a small lake on Phipps Island.

"Pulled out for Cordova just before noon, and 5 hours later were snug at our berth in Cordova Harbor.

"What a fantastic way to make a living."

CHAPTER

19

Two Nights And A Day

It can't be over 12 to 15 miles around the NE end of Hawkins Island to Windy and Cedar Bays on the NW side of that island, but it took us three days to get a Stakeout team tucked away there secretly. As I've said before, with such a vast area to police, and with so few "policemen," we *had* to use the element of secrecy.

Yes, I've said that 90 percent of those fishermen were honest, but, well, let me say it kindly, if one fisherman knows where a Stakeout crew is hidden, we had to assume that the entire fleet would soon know. So, we really worked at our "hidden spies" game.

F. M. J., Monday, July 26, 1965: "The *Shad* had brought Dick Smeltzer and Tom Wright back in from Eaglek Bay, so they needed a new location...So about 5:00 P.M., with the two boys and their tent, food, and gear aboard, we headed up Orca Inlet... We cruised easily, to give that glorious sun time to go to bed. It was still quite light, so we spent some time cruising outer Sheep Bay, making like we were just patrolling, then eased back across to Windy Bay, and anchored inside the markers about 8:30.

"I kept the boys down below and out of sight, while I cooked their supper. Two fish boats were anchored there also, so we just ate, and visited, and waited till 11:30 for them to leave. But they didn't leave. It was quite dark by then, so we made a couple trips ashore to fake putting the crew ashore, and then, with the boys back aboard on the off side of our ship, we pulled out with the *Brant*, stealthily, but not too stealthily, and were tied back at the Cordova dock by 2:30 or 3:00 A.M."

Cloak and dagger stuff? Sure, I suppose so. But we had to try, and, I must say, it was as much fun as playing Cops and Robbers when we were kids. And maybe that was all we were doing; but no one had given us a better idea.

F. M. J., Tuesday, July 27, 1965: "Back to the boat about 9:00 P.M., warmed up the engine and waited for my crew... We pulled out about 9:30, this time for Cedar Bay, a mile or so SW of Windy Bay, also on the NW side of Hawkins Island.

"It was quite dark by 11:30, as we approached the bay, and, running in a complete blackout, I was not quite able to read the details on my chart by starlight.

(As I write this, I note that it is curious that both times I hid a crew away in the midnight dusk, it was these same two men.)

"We sort of felt and sensed our way into Cedar Bay, watching our fathometer carefully, and anchored up well inside the markers, and waited awhile."

F. M. J., Wednesday, July 28, 1965: "We couldn't 'see' any other boats around, so just after midnight, I took the skiff and rowed up to the entrance of yet another lagoon, and looked around. All looked clear, so I rowed back to the ship, and we ferried the two boys and their gear ashore in two, heavy loads.

"I slipped out with the *Brant* about 1:00 A.M., and ran across to Sheep Bay, and anchored up behind the islands about 2:30. Although I felt for those two boys who were still scouting out a hidden camp site in the damp brush and in that midnight dusk, and getting their tent set up, I couldn't help them. So I crashed in my own warm bunk for a few hours...

"About 11:00 A.M., I rowed my dog, Cindy, ashore in that remarkably beautiful setting, then patrolled to the head of Sheep Bay, and finally turned for home about 1:00 P.M., and secure at our own berth a couple hours later."

Not a dramatic story, I think, but a simple picture of three days, or maybe I should say, two nights and a day in the life of a Protection-Boat Officer for the Alaska Department of Fish and Game, on Prince William Sound, a quarter of a century ago.

CHAPTER 20

Two Stories

All In The Day's Work

F. M. J., Friday, July 30, 1965: "Down to the boat to fill out my 'trip tickets.' Bob down with an FBI agent. They wanted me to run them across the inlet, looking for some stolen piling.

"I asked the agent, a quiet, well mannered man, 'Don't you fellows have more sinister crimes to deal with than a few stolen piling?'

"He smiled a gentle smile and replied. 'Oh, it's all part of the job. The theft of these piling do represent several thousands of dollars; and, it is an involved, interstate problem. We are best equipped to take care of it.'

"We found the stolen piling in a shallow cove across the inlet, and even some more. He knew where the thief was. He just needed to confirm the evidence. He took several pictures, and we returned to Cordova. Again, the FBI got their man."

I hide a couple of boys, on a dark night, on an island; and the next day, I'm working with the Federal Bureau Of Investigation. But, all in the day's work.

Loneliness At Port Etches

Continuing from my Journal: "Some other fishing areas were being closed, so Bob told me there was increased fishing pressure on Port Etches. Would I run down alone, for a few days, and police the area.

"I had fueled up on arrival, and my food supply was OK, so I headed out about 3:00 P.M., into a bit of a Sou'easter, for the 40-mile run. I really wanted to arrive after dark, so that, just in case someone *was* fishing after hours, I would have the element of surprise. But I was surprised at how easily that small ship moved as I kept coming back on the throttle. We were still making 5 knots, with the engine not much above idle.

"I suppose it did look a little curious to see this police boat, prowling slowly over the sea. For somewhere off Canoe Passage, or near there, I saw a small group of fishing boats, rafted together in a bite in the shore. A high-speed skiff came racing out; but he just circled the *Brant*, looking me over carefully. I smiled innocently, and waved, but there was no response. He was probably one of the 10 percent.

"It was dark as I slipped into Constantine Harbor, and dropped anchor inside the entrance. I rowed Cindy ashore, and then cruised the area with the skiff before heading for my warm bunk. It was 11:00 P.M."

F. M. J., Saturday, July 31, 1965: "But I was up at 2:00 A.M. to look over the harbor with my excellent binoculars. No apparent unlawful fishing, so I had an early breakfast, and then Cindy and I in my skiff, patrolled that entire inner bay, and then Port Etches with the *Brant*. I watched a pretty, little double ender make a good catch of around 750 fish, and then followed him to the big tender and checked licenses on several boats there.

"There is a lifting of the spirit in the camaraderie that builds when a number of boats and crews gather. I needed that in my often lonely job. "

F. M. J., Sunday, August 1, 1965: "A quiet, cloudy, but beautiful day. It was Sunday, so had a lazy breakfast, some reading and resting, and finally took the skiff on a two-hour cruise of this mile-wide, two-mile-long, most unique lagoon. I found a pair of small cabins, one almost rotted away, up at the NW corner on a wooded peninsula that was jutting into the lagoon from the north shore. I listened with my heart for their story, but the empty, silent rooms would not speak to me. Again the sadness of sharing, if but for a little while, the pathos of the sun-bleached skeletons of dreams that have died.

"Bob dropped from the sky aboard the chartered Gruman Goose about 3:30, and showed me the new closures—all of Montague Island, and the SE District, and the time cut to 12 hours a day on the little remaining; 6 A.M. to 6 P.M. I am to run for Port Gravina tomorrow.

"They flew away on their yellow wings, taking the thunder of their engines with them, and the silence folded in like the silver sea upon the wake of

The sun-bleached skeleton of a dream that has died.
Constantine Harbor. August 1, 1965.

my ship; and I felt curiously alone. I took my skiff and advised the four boats in the harbor, and then the *Brant* across Port Etches and advised six more.

"The death of a season? Was it a living thing then? It was only a block of time, designated by men. But it was gone. A quiet sadness holds me in its spell tonight."

CHAPTER

21

The Cloak Is Torn Away

F. M. J., Monday, August 2, 1965: "Cindy and I had a leisurely breakfast, and pulled out about 7:00 into an unusual, summer fog on Prince William Sound. (Well, dogs eat breakfast too. And Cindy was a gentle, Border Collie. She never wolfed her food down, but almost dined, daintily. She was a real lady, and a real friend. I *would* have been lonely without her.)

"About an hour and a half out, we spotted the Tender, *Sprig*, anchored up in outer Shelter Bay; so we swung alongside for coffee, and visit with Capt. 'Buck' Loomis and his crew."

Those Tender Captains were a special breed themselves. As well as boatmen, they were also administrators, Company Representatives, and most of all, Shipwrights. Not only were there the appurtenances of their ship to care for, but there were generators, and compressors, and winches, and reefer units, and hoists, and scales, and radios, and pumps, and plumbing, and electrical panels to care for. Capt. "Buck" Loomis appeared to be at ease in his many-faceted role.

Continuing F. M. J.: "Both of us on north together, about 10:30 for that strikingly beautiful, deep, green fiord that is called Port Gravina... Much of the fleet had congregated here, so it was a busy place...

"I anchored on the new closure line, as we had no markers out in that short time, and had a good lunch, and watched the fleet... This afternoon, we cruised the fleet, checking boats and licenses. A good visit with Bob Burnham and his crew on the *Isabell*, and with Bob Maxwell and his crew on the *Bear Cape*. These were real men, with the evident triple marks of real men, character, strength, and gentleness, that the sea builds in those who learn to walk in harmony with her.

"Bobbie Anderson flew over in the plane as I was looking into lovely, deep, little Comfort Cove, and radioed for me to also check Olsen Bay, as we no longer had stakeouts there.

"We anchored for the night on the south end of the closure line about 9:00 P.M... Light, scattered drizzle showers, but beautiful as always in that so unique way that superlatives fail to tell. The stirrings deep within defy anything so inadequate as words."

F. M. J., Tuesday, August 3, 1965: "Today we closed the season... The *Bear Cape* woke me at 7:00, asking about the new closure line in St. Matthew Bay. So we had our breakfast, and then set out to patrol Comfort Cove, Beartrap Bay (what a magnificent place), upper Port Gravina (watched

The M/V *Brant* at anchor in Comfort Cove, with the fishing vessel, F/V *Kee*, the evening before the poem "Prince William Sound, Alaska" was written.

30 seals sunbathing on the sand), Olsen Bay (a paradise where a big black bear was catching salmon), St. Matthew Bay (checked a fisherman), back across Port Gravina (where 12- to 14-foot sharks were ripping up the schools of salmon), and anchored opposite Parshas Bay for supper... Took pictures in Beartrap Bay of the so well-marked old and new high tide lines, a good 6 feet apart. What force beyond comprehension it had to take to shove several hundred square miles of towering mountains up that 6 feet, and hold them there. We tread upon these waters in awe and deep respect for the Author of that power.

"Bob flew over again this evening and radioed that the 'escapement' (number of fish getting on up to spawn) was not holding up, so they have closed the season in all Prince William Sound. I knew that the big tenders had the message, so would pass it on to the boats around, so I ran into Comfort Cove; so still and beautiful, and advised the boat *Kee* about the season end... We visited until 10:00 or so, and then I anchored off of them a bit for the night."

F. M. J., Wednesday, August 4, 1965: "We weighed anchor, and eased away from the comfort of Comfort Cove, with the *Kee* following, about 9:30 A.M., heading for home; home, that lovely word that we kept tucked safely away from our conscious, right-now, day-to-day thinking. Except for we two, and two fish boats I checked on the way out, the fleet was gone, most having battened down, upped anchor and rushed away very soon after the announcement that the season was ended had reached them. The announcement had 'torn the cloak away,' it was no longer needed. And so they had run for 'home,' even though it meant running late into the night."

And I understood that. They were out upon those waters to catch fish, to earn a living for the year in the short time given them. That meant long hours of hard work and intense concentration, and so they, and I too, had slipped a protective cloak around ourselves to protect us from the interference of the longing to be at home with our families. Our emotions could not carry both at the same time.

I remember the story of *Tinkerbell*, the 90-day, solo sailing of that tiny, tiny, 13-foot sailboat across the Atlantic Ocean to England some years ago. As his voyage progressed, over the long weeks, the world, especially the boating world, began to notice.

Alaska's sea-washed mountains.
Prince William Sound, Alaska. August 4, 1965.

At the time, I believe it was the smallest sailboat to cross that ocean.

From time to time, aircraft and British Navy craft would check on him. But in his own words, the most extremely difficult time came, two or three weeks from his destination, when the Navy came out, and there was his wife, standing by the rail, waving.

A real part of him incongruously resented seeing her there. He was not ready to let that cloak go. And when they had gone, and he was left, alone again upon the empty sea, with weeks yet to sail on alone, he had to make a valiant struggle to pull the cloak around him again. His mind, and his emotions could not survive without its protection. Oh yes, I understood that well.

But, although I well understood that, I had not, myself, been so long away, and, I had yet a job to do, sweeping the area to make sure there were no stragglers who had unknowingly, or knowingly, missed the announcement. But oh yes, I understood that well.

Oh, I know that the emotions, set free by the season end, the going home, were filling my very being; but Neptune had also crowned this time with a glorious day beyond description. The light breeze, with its light but short chop, together with the angle of the morning sun, made the curvature of this ball on which we live stand out in a rare clarity.

And all this charged my mind and pen to copy down the words of the poem, "Prince William Sound, Alaska" (see Chapter 12) that came in such a rushing flood that I could hardly write legibly at all. I have written many poems, but I did not write, or compose this one; I could only copy it down.

And as I did, I saw that there were six lines in the first verse, seven in the second, five in the third, and four in the fourth.

"That's OK," I quickly thought, "I'll fix that later," and scribbled on. But the next day, at home, as I went to type it up, I could change not a thing. It was right the first time, and so it remains.

" 'Prince William Sound, Alaska,'... discovered at sea, under a brilliant, northern sun."

Our bows were pointed toward home.

CHAPTER 22

Plaiting Myself Back Together

As the Polynesian navigators well knew, after a long voyage the loneliness of command at sea demanded that one spend some time just "plaiting one's self back together."

So the *Brant* dozed contentedly at her berth, and I just ambled about in the restful security of harbor and home, and let the simple, uncomplicated events of this fishing village life guide my days.

F. M. J., Friday, August 6, 1965: "...We drove down to the ocean dock this evening and watched a small (150- to 200-ft) Japanese ship loading salmon eggs, a prized delicacy in Japan.

"I asked to go aboard and see the engine. The engineer and I did not speak each other's language, but we knew ships, we knew engines, we knew the sea; we communicated. And he was, and had a reason to be, proud of his spotless engine room. The big, six cylinder diesel was obviously a direct reversible, and around 650 hp She really was a neat little ship."

In the meantime, some local townspeople had loaned some fishing poles to some of the crewmen. They were delightedly pulling in occasional bottom fish.

But—the law. I'm glad that I don't remember what Fish and Game Official came down to spoil the fun.

"Those crewmen are not licensed to fish here; they must stop," he informed the interpreter. So they stopped.

But that dilemma was soon solved. The owners of the fishing poles took them back, and kept on fishing, legally, of course, and threw each catch aboard, to the delight of everyone, especially those Japanese crewmen. International relations at the grass roots level, or should I say, at sea level.

F. M. J., Saturday, August 7, 1965: "Alma and I down to the harbor at an early 7:00 A.M. We boarded the *Shad* with all the permanent Fish and Game people, their wives and kids, for the annual Fish and Game Picnic at Boswell Bay on Hinchinbrook Island, 15 or so miles south down Orca Inlet. It was a fabulous, clear, hot, sunny, summer day, here, on the eastern edge of deep Prince William Sound where she joins the copper sands.

"We picked wild strawberries, some a gallon or more, got gloriously sunburned, and played softball, barefoot, in the sun-warmed sand."

The entrance to the bay is marked by a number of massive, stone pillars, maybe 50 to 100 feet high. They were nearly covered with the nests of gulls, murrelets, and other birds; and all nests were occupied. When we entered, Capt. Curran held the

Shad at slow bell, her engines speaking only a subdued, soothing rumble. The birds nervously held their nests, as we slid between those pillars, with most of the 30 or so passengers out on the open well-deck of the *Shad*.

And then Capt. Curran pulled the cord on the ship's whistle. The blast sent a thousand birds into the sky over that small ship. The hilarious havoc can only best be described by the words of a song, "...darn those seagulls; it's a good thing cows don't fly."

But there was no mutiny. Capt. Curran was loved; and the "family" was together, building that special bonding that only a family on a picnic together, can build.

I suspect that a State Vessel can no longer be used for such a purpose, and maybe correctly so, but if so, I can see that only as a loss. A nebulous, immeasurable thing, I know, but the loss of the special bonding that occurred on those Fish and Game family picnics, can only show as a debit on the balance sheet between the public, and those special Alaska State employees.

A couple of weeks later, I realized that I, myself, had a debt to pay. Jeanette Bailey, the Office Secretary, although in no way obligated to help me with my reports and other paper work, had, in her gentle but efficient way, helped me many times.

So I invited her and her husband, Bill, and their kids, to go with Alma and me on a picnic and fishing trip up to Deep Bay one evening aboard the *Brant*. They were all fine people, and most appreciative, but I can't resist telling a bit of a story on Bill. He was set up by fate.

Alma looked like a quiet, little, innocent housewife. She did not look like an outdoorsman, a skilled or gifted sport fisherman. Bill was both. But, Alma was her father's daughter, and so had inherited that mysterious, but very real quality, "Fisherman's Luck." I rigged a crab ring, and hung it over the side. Jeanette sat and watched. The kids played. But Bill and Alma set to serious fishing, one off the port side, and one off the starboard.

Alma started catching fish; Bill caught nothing. After a while, muttering as he rebaited his hook; he stepped over to fish off Alma's side. No one said anything, but after a bit, she hauled in to rebait, and quietly stepped over to the other side, and lowered her hook. She continued catching fish. Bill continued catching nothing, or only a few.

I don't know how many times this reversal of positions took place, but it was several. And I'm sorry, Bill Bailey, to tell this story on you, but I know that your sense of humor will come to the rescue. No question about it, Brother, on the average, men will out fish women, no question. But now you know why you did not that one time. You were set up by fate

No one in Cordova thought that taking these people on that fishing trip aboard that State Vessel was improper at all. And where it was definitely never abused, I don't think it was. But, sadly, I'm sure one cannot do that anymore either.

Bill and Jeanette Bailey and their kids were a mighty fine family. I remember them all with a fond, fond memory. They contributed much to the "plaiting of myself back together."

CHAPTER 23

Eshamy

[*UNITED STATES COAST PILOT*, US Dept. of Commerce, N.O.A.A., National Ocean Service: "*Eshamy Bay,* between Point Nowell and Crafton Island, affords anchorage only for small craft in 8 to 11 fathoms, in the small cove back of the islands and rocks in the SE corner of the bay. The better entrance is through the middle of the deep narrow channel between the small islands and the E shore. *Eshamy Lagoon* extends W from Eshamy Bay, but its foul entrance with strong currents makes it inaccessible for strangers."]

Such are the terse words of this really incredibly informative publication. And for the mariner, they are enough. But they do not tell of Eshamy. Yet, shall I?

Again, as that famous poet, T. S. Elliot said so long ago (or was it just yesterday?), "Words are so inadequate."

How does one really tell about Eshamy? Where are the unworn words with which to paint for others a portrait that would show her magic, her mystery, her Spirit, her spell? How can I sound, here, with these inadequate words, the silent music she sings to all who have ever known her, if but for only a little while?

How many times, over the long but so swiftly flowing years since I met her, have I mentioned Eshamy in a conversation, and someone listening, would smile wistfully, and respond, "Oh yes, Eshamy." They knew; they knew.

As we have said before, Prince William Sound is so strikingly beautiful that words do fail, but it is a severe beauty. And yes, Eshamy is very much a part of Prince William Sound. But Eshamy had a gentle side; she comforted too. And though I spent much of that long summer cruising those deep and magnificent waters, I probably saw less than 10 percent of Prince William Sound. But I was graced to know Eshamy.

So let me simply tell my story, and trust the Author of communication to surround my words with a Spirit that tells as mere words cannot tell.

F. M. J., Sunday, August 8, 1965: "We just laid around this day, and nursed our sunburn, and talked plans for buying or building a 'home base,' 'somewhere'...

"...Bob called this evening, and wants me to run to Eshamy for a couple weeks to check setnetters. 'Alma's job at the cannery is finished,' he said, 'You need a cook; take her along.'"

F. M. J., Monday, August 9, 1965: "Gathered gear, and groceries, and fueled the boat this morning... Streamguard, Irving Warner needed a ride to Eshamy, so he, Alma, and I and Cindy, our Border Collie, pulled out near noon in a quiet, rainy, cloudy day.

"I had thought to go straight across the middle of that inland sea to the Naked Islands, but the SE wind really piped up; and off Knowles Head it got pretty rough. I didn't say anything to either of my two passengers, but I thought to myself, 'The State is not paying me to fight this,' so I swung right to cut behind Goose Island. My passengers expressed their relief.

"Holding close outside Bligh Island and Bligh Reef, to stay in the lee of Goose Island and Knowles Head, protecting us from that SE storm, we ran on into Columbia Glacier and again hauled out a dozen, 10-pound chunks of that ancient ice for our meats and vegetables. It was raining hard, but somehow the storm only amplified the awesome beauty of the massive wall of that frozen river relentlessly trying to push back the sea. Ah, but what can win against the sea? The mountain cannot, given the sea enough time. How then can a snowflake? For that is all that the ice really is, one snowflake pressed into another.

"Our detour had run us late, so we ran around again into beautiful Billie's Hole, in Long Bay, and anchored for the night about 7:30. Our cook prepared a yachtsman's, excellent steak dinner; and we dined, as the night and the sea and the mountains wrapped their spell around us."

F. M. J., Tuesday, August 10, 1965: "The spirit of the early dawn had our cook up before 5:00. The aroma of hot coffee had two men soon following. It was a cloudy, but beautiful, clear morning. Across the mirrored pond, three black bears were catching salmon at the head of the lagoon. So we all three slipped into the skiff, paddled over to the shore, and then walked up to within 100 yards of two of them, who just wandered off, and then turned and looked at us. *We* were the intruders; we knew that.

"Back aboard our little ship, we cruised gently out from that incredibly protected place, through that narrow, deep, stone walled channel, into a calm, still outer bay about 8:30. We were mildly surprised to meet some low ground swells from the Pacific as we cleared Glacier Island; and then we met a sharp chop from the west wind. Still, it was an easy, 5-hour run to beautiful Eshamy Lagoon. I had met her, so briefly, once before, but I believe it is not stretching poetic license to say, I sensed her welcoming smile.

"And as we ducked into that gouge on the southern shore, and around the point of that narrow peninsula, jutting down from the north shore, we suddenly left the sea behind us, and stepped into her comforting, welcoming stillness and peace. Someone closed a soundproof door behind us. I did not miss the deepening of the silence emanating from my two passengers.

"Jerry Baron, a seasoned veteran now, and Ray Vroble, both headquartering in our R and R cabin on the peninsula, were here to meet us. Irving, who was to help John David Solf for a while, had brought along a stuffed turkey. So Ray ran him up the 3 miles or so to the head of the lagoon to John David's cabin, where they put it to roast. (The ADF& G didn't pay all that well; but a man with a full stomach, and having fun at his work, never complains.)

"We visited with our special friend, Jerry, awhile and then he ran us up to John David's cabin in the

Wahoo. A weir, a sort of wooden fence, had been built across the small river that tumbled down a few thousand feet from Eshamy Lake. The weir forced the returning salmon to go through a narrow opening where a close estimate of the count could be taken. We walked up the few hundred yards to the weir and watched hundreds of those big, Red, or Sockeye salmon working through that weir. We took the dipnet there and lifted a beauty out for our dinner tomorrow.

"And then we met back at John David's for that roast turkey dinner.

"Our candlelight and wine were a kerosene lantern and icy spring water; but three men of the sea, a mountain man, and a woman, dined, really dined, and shared such rich conversation. All were sharp minds, but John David's was also deep and thoughtful. Still, his uncomplicated, gentle speech could communicate fully and easily to every level of intellect. No one who knew him would think of calling him John or David. He was always called John David; and I'm not sure that any of us knew why. He was most comfortable to be around, yet no one spoke of him casually, or lightly, but rather as they spoke of Eshamy, as one would speak of a very special friend, who knew you to the core, and loved you anyway, with an unfeigned love.

"John David was a biologist for the ADF & G, and had spent several summers, and, I believe, a winter or two at 'John David's' cabin, doing special research on those unique Sockeyes.

"As I write of him now, I realize that that very real, yet really indescribable Spirit that flows with

Eshamy, also flowed with John David. Did he baptize her with that Spirit; or did she baptize him; or did the Creator of them both bring them together? However it came to be, those of us who have been privileged to "touch just the hem of their garments," received something into our souls, a something that, even now, these long years later, can be tapped as needed for peace, and comfort, and healing."

Oh, there was a special anointing upon this man, yes, but he was very much of this earth too. The altar of practicality had to be served at times; and he was able, like the time he had to kill a bear.

It is nothing new, of course, for it to become absolutely necessary to kill a bear that has moved into a camp. Soft and cuddly though they may appear to be, they are really not very intelligent, and are very brazen; one might even say, they are very narrow-minded and self-centered, with "no upbringing" at all.

A small 200 or 300 pound bear had moved in on his turf. For awhile, he appreciated the company. But like some people, the bear kept moving on in. The outhouse was damaged, the garbage pit became a shambles, supplies stored around the cabin were seriously damaged. The bear had to go; but he wouldn't go. Yells, rocks, buckets of water—he wouldn't go.

I don't know if John David kept a gun there or not. But one day, his patience worn thin, he stepped out onto his porch. The bear was rooting around in stored things under the porch. There was a 2-pound hammer lying there. So as the bear backed out from under the porch, John David hit him on the head with that hammer—hard. The bear fell, not moving.

At first, he thought he had killed it, but then he could see that it was still breathing. I don't think John David was one to panic, but any woodsman knows that a wounded bear is a terror to encounter. So he grabbed his water bucket, stepped down beside the bear, and managed to get its head and nose pointed down into that water. The bear weakly struggled for a few minutes, and then lay still.

But the dilemma was not yet over. He couldn't have the carcass of a dead bear rotting at his doorstep, and he couldn't drag it away. I don't recall how he did move it, but it was some ingenious way of rigging some poles, and prying and rolling it over the bank and into the lagoon, where the tide floated it away.

I don't think John David wanted to kill anything. But when it was demanded, he was able to sacrifice on that altar of practicality. It was just that only a John David Solf could make that sacrifice in such a specially unique way.

Eshamy might well be called a Sockeye paradise. There was that large, quiet inner lagoon, with a fresh stream pouring into the upper end. The salmon could school up there, resting from the sea, and getting a taste again of fresh water. There was that rushing, but easily passable stream, calling them home to the place of their birth. There was the 2-mile long Eshamy Lake at the end of the trail, with its acres of gravel beds where they were born, and where Sockeye really like to spawn.

I walked up the trail, one day, and took John David's Arkansas Traveler, a simple, flat-bottomed, aluminum punt, across the 2-mile lake to its head, and watched the mating dance of spawning salmon for an hour and a half.

A large female, great with child, would be patiently circling, and defending, her own dished out place in the gravel under that clear water, waiting, waiting. A male would be waiting off to one side also. When the birthing pangs would come upon her, she would begin a curious quivering. The male would sense the impending drama. And as the moment of birthing overwhelmed her, she would squirt out a stream of eggs; and with an incredible precision, the male would rush to her side, and squirt out his sperm upon those eggs. The fertilized eggs would settle to the bottom, and nestle into the protection of the gravelly stones.

It was a moving drama; and I very nearly lost track of time. But, though I saw no bears there, I suddenly realized that I was in *their* realm. Something warned me to leave, now. I almost ran to the boat, back across that mountain lake where the almost totally unseen drama of re-creation was taking place beneath those cold, still waters, and walked back down the trail.

By the time I reached the weir, I had almost forgotten about bears. So as I walked out upon the weir, I didn't believe, for a few seconds, that that big, black thing, half hidden under the lower edge of the weir, was the back of a black bear. But before I could turn and run, the bear smelled me, and came out from under that weir in an explosion of water, and thrashed away across that small river. He was obviously terrified. But if he had asked, I'd have to have admitted that I was a little scared myself.

As long as we are telling bear stories, we might as well fill in two more here. Oh, we did our work; Jerry patrolling with his cabin skiff, and I with my little shore boat. But we found time to go gunkholing and looking for bears too.

With Jerry directing, he, Alma, and I in my little skiff quietly cruised back into some smaller lagoons within the larger one. With the wilderness wrapping us in its complete and perfect shroud, we found ourselves, in our little boat, headed for a gravelly shore a thousand feet away. Off to our right, and a thousand feet down the beach, a big, black bear was ambling along. We shut off the motor, and let the boat coast toward that beach.

Bears have very poor eyesight, and the sound of small outboard motors, especially some distance off, was no threat, they had learned. As we coasted toward that beach, and that bear walked up that beach, it soon became apparent that we would reach the same spot at the same time.

The sense of drama overcame our very real fears; we waited. I don't think that big, black bear was 20 feet away as the bow of that skiff crunched lightly into the gravel. He was totally unaware of our presence until that moment. But the coiled springs of his powerful legs unwound. He whirled to the right and charged up a very steep bank 10 or 15 feet high, and into the brush with a series of grunts and puffs, and with a stream of _____ jetting him on. Oh, that could have been dangerous, we knew that, but I would so much like to share that story again with Jerry. We have forgotten the fear. But I know our laughter would roar.

We eased around through those hidden islands to another small stream, and beached the boat on its small, gravel bar. Red salmon were working up the 20- to 40-foot wide, shallow stream, often with their backs out of water. I looked over once to see Cindy, our dog, pick up a 4 or 5 pound salmon and start for shore. I made her put it back.

But across that shallow stream was a low, 8 or 10 foot, steep bank, topped with brush. There was a well worn trail where bears had slid down to catch salmon. One or two hundred feet up the creek, we could hear the roar of a waterfall. I was carrying the .30-06 rifle. Alma and Jerry, carrying the cameras, were trying to find a way up to that waterfall. A huge bear, unaware of our presence, came sliding down that trail. I was some distance up the creek myself, so I hollered to Alma and Jerry to bring the cameras, as I started back toward the bear. When I glanced back to see if they were coming, I was startled, and,

I suppose, mildly irritated to see them running the opposite way.

We all three could have done some shooting. But I suppose that the fact that mine could have been with a powerful rifle, and theirs with but their cameras, had its influence on their actions. I never shot the bear; but neither did they. My later complaints were ignored.

And then there was Tish. A small, but independent cub had attached itself to the R and R cabin. Jerry had befriended it by throwing out table scraps.

I don't know if that baby whined one day, or not, but Jerry was certain that that baby was hungry. So he borrowed my skiff, and my big dipnet, and ran up to a creek and dipped out six or eight salmon, and brought them back for his "pet."

I never thought, at the time, to ask any higher official in the Alaska Dept. of Fish and Game if that was illegal, improper, or even wasteful. And today, I wouldn't care what the answer would be. It's a cute story; that's all that matters now.

F. M. J., Thursday, August 12, 1965: "...Beautiful, though mostly cloudy, summer day. Jerry ran to Pigot Bay for a couple barrels of fuel, but the *Shad* was out, picking them all up... I took my skiff and ran out to check set-netters, but there were none in the water. I covered up to and including Falls Bay, the moving camera of my mind recording, sometimes in awe, the magnificence of that scenery.

"Finally met set-net fisherman, Dan Thomas, who informed me that, due to the dwindling supply, the cannery had stopped taking fish, effectively ending the season.

"...This evening, John David, Irving, and Jerry came for an excellent, beef roast dinner, served out on the after deck of our 'Bristol Bay Yacht.' No one spoke of her, as I remember, but Eshamy approved. I know that the enveloping flow of her Spirit enriched our conversation in a silent, subtle, yet sweet and penetrating way...

"The *Shad* came in about 8:30, picking up empty oil drums... Cindy had another attack of apparently, severely itching feet."

It was a few weeks later that I learned the cause of that poor animal's agony. There is a specie of large jellyfish, with long, flowing threads hanging down from the body. The jellyfish has exuded an oil or jelly-like material on those threads. Some say that there are thousands of minuscule hooks imbedded in that material. But others insist that it is some kind of slow acting, acid-like ingredient. In any case, a jellyfish had become stranded on the shore and died there. The dog had innocently walked on those threads at low tide. Several hours later, the chemical action began on her feet; they were on fire, or at least she thought they were.

She charged around the deck, lay down, whining, then leaped up and charged around the deck again, finally leaping over the side and swimming for shore. We could hear her crying and thrashing around up in the brush and darkness. I think it was nearly an hour before that fire subsided, and we were able to bring an exhausted, pitiable pet back aboard.

But the story of the "Fire Jellyfish" (I don't know what their real name is) does not end there. Fishermen are very aware of the danger, and so are watchful for those insidious strands that might cling to their nets. But once in a while, they miss, and some of that material gets on their hands, as they are busily hauling in their catch. And then, misery of miseries, if a man has relieved himself over the side with those hands, a few hours later, and for an hour or so, he could truly believe that the fires of hell itself had a grip on him, you know where. But, understandably, usually, those fishermen were very, very careful.

F. M. J., Friday, August 13, 1965: "...Bob had said, over the radio this morning, to break down the camp and bring all the gear in to Cordova. We surveyed our job, and decided, *tomorrow*, we'll really tear into it. Then we took the *Brant* up to John David's cabin... Jerry and Alma fished with their poles, and I took that walk up to Eshamy Lake... When I returned, I found that she had caught a big, bright Sockeye, so we had that for supper after we ran back to 'our' end of the lagoon. Again, as that Dutch Stewardess, Renee', had said, 'What an experience.'"

F. M. J., Saturday, August 14, 1965: "...Quite heavy rain most of the day, but we had a job to do. Human beings are such packrats, so it took most of the day for Jerry, Alma, and me to gather that moun-

The proud Patrol Craft for the Alaska Department of Fish and Game, becomes a common freight boat. And the "First Officer" of that Patrol Craft....
August 14, 1965

tain of gear, tubs, utensils, barrels, even a gasoline-powered washing machine, pack them all down to the beach, and lighter it all out to the *Brant* with Jerry's Cabin Skiff. I must say, it really looked incongruous to see that washing machine lashed down in a corner on the after deck of that 'Police Boat'...

"...A real storm out in the sound, with some whipping in here with gusts, heavy rain showers, and even some ground swells...

"Jerry picked a half gallon of blueberries... We ran up to John David's cabin this evening for rich conversation, and a fine dinner of fresh, Sockeye salmon, and fresh, blueberry cobbler. Life is full tonight."

Eshamy

The M/V *Brant* at anchor near the abandoned Indian Village of Kiniklek. Note the washing machine lashed down on the after deck. August 17, 1965.

F. M. J., Sunday, August 15, 1965: "A sort of day off... Met Bob by radio (relaying through the *Shad*, somewhere out on the Sound) on schedule at 10:00. He said not to hurry in—so...."

F. M. J., Monday, August 16, 1965: "...Up early to listen to the marine forcast. 'Winds SSE 20 to 40 knots;' I agree, no hurry...

"...Alma, Cindy and I finally headed out with our loaded, little ship, about noon. There was a light chop, drizzle, and fog. We set a course, north through the fog, for [yet another] Cedar Bay; and 3 hours later, came out of the heavy fog just south of Fairmount Island, or only 5 degrees off.

"We slipped on into Cedar Bay in heavy drizzle and fog, and anchored up in a beautiful cove, protected (again) by an island. A huge mama bear and two cubs were searching for salmon at the head of the lagoon; and then a yearling cub, and then another. 'Lord, can we not stay; must we return?'"

The Russian Orthodox Church at Kiniklek.
August 17, 1965.

F. M. J., Tuesday, August 17, 1965: "...Ran to the abandoned Indian Village of Kiniklek, and stopped to explore awhile. We found a number of wooden grave markers, and but one building yet standing— the partially tumbled down, 8 feet by 10 feet, Russian Orthodox Church. The silence spoke its wordless message to our hearts...

"...Finally away around noon, heading for 'home.' A pair of killer whales escorted us all the way from

Valdez Arm to the Channel Islands, under a beautiful, summer sky. It is good to be home."

But I must speak yet once more of Eshamy. When we sailed away from her, I have no recollection that we said goodbye to her. Perhaps we were not fully cognizant of what we were really leaving. Or the press of new adventure held our attention.

But now, looking back down that long trail of years, I am poignantly aware of two, deep impressions upon our souls, Eshamy, and John David Solf.

John David died that winter, or maybe a winter or two later, so he can speak to us no more. He had fallen through the ice; and though the *Shad* and her crew were only a few hundred feet, or yards away, because of the ice, it was some time before they could effect a rescue. Perhaps they did not know then of hypothermia, but though he was alive when they finally got him into the warm cabin of the *Shad*, he had been so chilled, waiting in that frigid water, that the internal fire that makes us all "warm blooded animals," had gone out. He died there, in some unnamed cove, in some unknown corner of the sea.

But Eshamy, whose Spirit he shared, lives on, and bathes the souls of all who enter there in that anointing oil.

And we, we who were anointed there so long ago, still understand very well, that wistful smile when she is spoken of; and we understand the depth behind the quiet words, "Oh yes, Eshamy."

CHAPTER
24

Work—or Play

We unloaded, and stowed away in the warehouse, that small shipload of Eshamy gear; we caught up on our mail, and the latest Fish and Game news (gossip?); we rested in the steady, protected peace of the harbor, and let the solid land wash our sea legs away. After a voyage, it just takes some time to settle us back into the routine and flow of living on the shore, and among the people of the land.

F. M. J., Saturday, August 21, 1965: "...Son-in-law, Bill phoned today that daughter, Judy, was very ill and needed her mother; so I rushed her out to the Airport at mile 13, for the noon, PNA (Pacific Northern Airlines) flight to Anchorage..."

F. M. J., Sunday, August 22, 1965: "... Lazily slept in late, and then ambled down to the boat, and 'Vasilandoed' around the docks in the beautiful, hot sun, and visited with fishermen..."

But it has been well written, "A boat in the harbor is safe, but that is *not* what boats were built for," and so:

The M/V *Brant*, peacefully at anchor in the still, incomparably lovely, west end of "Canoe Passage," Hawkins Island. August 24, 1965.

F. M. J., Tuesday, August 24, 1965: "And still another, beautiful, warm summer day... A lazy, late breakfast, and ambled down to the boat with all my gear. The two Sport Fish Biologists, Ed Jones, and Lynn Nutter again, helped me shop for groceries. We loaded all their gear, and finally slipped our moorings, and left our sleepy berth about 3:00 P.M., towing, of course, my shore boat, but also their 16 ft *Arkansas Traveler*, and anchored up inside the west end of Canoe Passage about 5:30.

"Our good cook, Ed, prepared our supper, and then the two of them paddled out to measure and count a creek, while I cleaned up my galley... We all just read for awhile in the still, still evening, as the slowly flooding tide whispered around the hull."

It is curious that now, so many years later, that I notice how many times we sailed late in the day, or even evening. We seldom ran at night, but such was the easy, gentle, but steady flow of life there, that we just sailed "when it was time to go." Like eating our meals when we got hungry, instead of the regimented 7:00—12:00—7:00 of the business world. Oh, I know, the business world must have a schedule, must be regimented to a great degree, just to operate efficiently with one another. But I sincerely believe that that uncomplicated flow of life, there, on Prince William Sound, and the Copper Sands, left much energy free to accomplish the prodigious work of harvesting food from the sea. The engines of life did not wear out so swiftly.

But back to Canoe Passage:

Again I quote from the terse words of the *COAST PILOT*: Pacific and Arctic Coasts Alaska; Cape Spencer To Beaufort Sea; Page 61: "Hawkins Island, about 20 miles long, and mountainous, is divided by Canoe Passage, about eight miles from its SW end; the passage is no longer navigable."

Old-timers told me, that before the uplift from the earthquake, small boats could, and did, occasionally, shortcut through there on their runs between Cordova and the Sound. The next day we ran east, up the passage a couple miles, as I remember, in one of our small boats and found the last mile or so indeed impassable, even for canoes. Rushes and grass were quickly filling in the little water there. I suspect that by now, there is no longer even any tidal flow there, and so finally, north and south Hawkins Islands are truly joined as one.

Who cares? I care, and I know that there are others who care. The Creator has His reasons for making the vast, geologic changes that only He can make. But I think that He understands our very real sense and feeling of the loss to us, of even that one, small, almost unknown channel of the sea.

F. M. J., Wednesday, August 25, 1965: "All of us up at 7:00 into a beautiful (mountain type) summer day... Lynn and I paddled over to measure and count a stream before breakfast... Later, all three of us ran on up the navigable portion of the passage, and counted and measured a couple more streams, and then had to explore on up to the actual passage, which was [as I've said] clearly impassable, even for canoes... We put both of our 5 hp outboards on that *Arkansas Traveler*. What a hotrod. (Well, the boy in us had to have *some* expression.)

"...This afternoon we ran back up to the Forest Service cabin (free for any to use) and carried that lightweight, aluminum punt the half mile up the trail to 'Lake No. 1' We set a test fish net (almost invisible, monofilament, with varying sized mesh), and Lynn and I trolled for trout. We didn't catch anything, but Ed caught a couple near the outlet. What a life! Still, someone had to 'officially' gather that information.

"Back aboard, I caught up in my log, while the boys checked another stream. Then Ed cooked an excellent evening meal for us; we dined, and listened to our radio, and read, and watched the dull gold and amber light, from the sun over China, fade across the oiled waters of the flooding tide."

F. M. J., Thursday, August 26, 1965: "...All up early into a beautiful morning... I rowed Cindy ashore, and then just paddled around while Ed fixed our breakfast... All of us out in the *Traveler*, and ran down the coast a mile or so and surveyed a few streams... After lunch, the boys ran down the coast again, but I stayed aboard and caught up in my log and reports, and considered a couple poems, stirred by the stillness, and beauty here (I had moved the *Brant* further inside to a smaller cove), and because I miss my family... The boys didn't finish their day 'til after 7:00."

F. M. J., Friday, August 27, 1965: "...And yet *another* still and beautiful day... The boys ran down the coast again in their small boat, and I cleaned up the *Brant*... Weighed anchor about noon, and ran down the coast about 3 miles, and anchored offshore. They came out for lunch. ...The Sound was almost a mirror, and the mountains were vying with each other for the greatest display of glory on that rugged skyline... We ran back to snuggle deep inside Canoe Passage for the night..."

F. M. J., Saturday, August 28, 1965: "...Our first cloudy day in some time... We ran to Anderson Bay, picked our way carefully in through the shallow, rocky, and twisting channel, and were anchored well inside by noon... Rain this evening."

F. M. J., Sunday, August 29, 1965: "...A rainy, yet beautiful, still day... The powerful mountains to the NW, standing tall and clear in the sun, looked especially impregnable and dominating, looking at them out from under our cloud ceiling. ...The boys went counting, and I worked on my little ship, and wrote the following poetic essay, in the form of a letter to my family:

[This portion of excerpt from my journal, as well as parts of several more that appear in the rest of this book, appeared also in my book, *ISLANDS OF EXPERIENCE*. But they were in that book because of their poetic expression. I publish them here because they tell the story. To leave them out would mean that a part of *this* story would be missing. We can't have that.]

A Sailor's Two Loves

"There is a sweet and gently painful loneliness on the sea, somewhat akin to nostalgia, and although on this trip aboard the M/V *Brant* it was generally well suppressed by the company of two biologists, both lively and friendly extroverts, these men would sometimes leave the ship for half a day at a time, and the full awareness of the sailor's loneliness would have the free course to come to the surface and be known.

"And so it was, one long Alaskan afternoon, in the heart of this mountain-torn sea, as I sat down in the silence, alone, to write a letter in:

> "Anderson Bay
> Hinchinbrook Island
> Prince William Sound
> Alaska
> August 29, 1965

"My Beloved Family,

The thunder of silence is almost deafening, and would be so were it not for the occasional dampening effect of the sound of a raven's call, or the cry of a gull, or the patter of rain drops on the deck, or the rush of an almost imperceptible ground swell on a low gravel bar.

Why is it we find it so necessary, so often, to disturb that perfect harmony of all sound, the silence, with artificial sounds of our own, which at best are but distortions of the silence?

Only when we stand in the silence, alone, can we be really aware of standing at the meeting place of two eternities, the past and the future, and look at the mountains as they were in the long past, and will be in the distant future, but mostly as they are, here, now, in the only reality, the thundering, powerfully eternal, and silent present.

And suddenly I am aware that I miss my family; that the magnetic bond that ties a family together has been pulling its slight, but persistent, elastic, yet indestructible strand; and the burden, like a pail of water carried in the hand, becomes increasingly heavy to bear the longer it is borne.

Yet through the mist that shrouds, but never completely hides the future, I see myself in the warmth and glow and joy of my family; and I hear another sound, the voice of a siren, the call of the sea; and I know I will have to leave that love for another even before I have returned to my own.

And so it is with those who love the sea: cursed, or blessed (who is to say?) with two loves, where the wonder of each is somehow magnified by possession of the other; and the sailor finds himself with one plea: love him, and let him love you. His love is sweeter, greater, more to be cherished for his other love; and he needs the silence and distance of the sea wherein that love can grow and expand and show itself to him in purity and in power.

>Love,
>Dad Nichols
>Capt. M/V *Brant*

"...The boys finished their work about 1:00, we had lunch, and pulled out about 2:30 for the three-hour run north to Simpson Bay, and anchored in the north end of the SE arm about 5:30. The penetrating beauty of these mountain-walled coves still catch us into breathless awe... There were three or four private boats sport fishing for Silvers, so Ed and Lynn whipped out their own gear and started casting...

"About 9:30, I rowed Cindy ashore in the dark, and oh so still night, and watched my oars stir a whirlwind of phosphorus fire at each stroke, then drip a stream of liquid fire as they swung forward. The wake from my skiff was like a thousand stars; and near the shore the streaking comets just beneath the surface were Silver Salmon igniting the phosphorus into a stream of fire. What incredible beauty in the stillness of a dark, dark night."

F. M. J., Monday, August 30, 1965: "The boys were up at 4:30, and by the time I joined them at 8:00, they had eleven beautiful Silvers. ...Cloudy,

Work—or Play

The mountain, the sea, and a Captain's best friend.
Prince William Sound, Alaska. Summer, 1965.

and not a breath of air... Weighed anchor about 9:00, and were tied at the Cordova dock by 10:30."

As I look back down the years, to that rare and unique time, and watch those virile young men, standing on the deck of a Patrol Boat for the Alaska Department of Fish and Game, catching Silver Salmon for the folks at home, I still cannot always distinguish the work from the play. And then I realize; it doesn't really matter; it doesn't make any difference at all.

CHAPTER 25

A Fragrant Memory

The crab season was starting, but my Son's family, and my daughter's family, and my wife were all in Anchorage. And the deep emotional drive that had given us, "A Sailor's Two Loves," was still with me.

I don't think I've ever had a finer boss than Bobbie Anderson, and not just because he was good to me. As I have said, he was no pussycat. He was good-natured, but he could be tough, resolved, and right. But I had lived on that marvelous little ship for four long months; I needed to touch my family. Though young, Bobbie had the wisdom to see that.

"Go ahead and take three days now," he said; "The last salmon run of the season, the Silvers, will be beginning at Bering River in a week. When you get back, we'll send you down to Police that." So I flew to Anchorage on the next PNA Flight.

Although not really a part of this story of the sea, I must include a few words from my Journal that tell the rich and lovely relationship this Dad had with his beautiful son.

We had a cabin on a five-acre piece of wilderness that brushed the shore of a small lake named, officially now, "Lloyd's Pond." After he died when that tugboat sank under him a year later, I took the legal steps to have that name officially applied to that small lake. Both the State Board, and the National Board of Geographic Place Names, gave their official sanction.

Twenty-five miles due north of Anchorage, but 50 miles by road, lies a string of lakes, Big Lake, Mirror Lake, and Flat Lake. Just north of Mirror Lake, lies Lloyd's Pond. All are connected by narrow channels.

F. M. J., Wednesday, September 1, 1965: "...Back to Lloyd's job about 4:30 P.M., and helped him warehouse some things. Then we loaded our eight-foot aluminum pram, the three hp Evinrude, and some gas, and headed for Big Lake about 7:00. We bought a few cans of beans and other prepared foods in Eagle River, and then drove to Nolfi's cabin on the south shore of Big Lake. It was very dark as we launched our tiny, tiny boat. But two boys were having a truly great time...

"Making maybe a maximum speed of 4 or 5 knots, that little boat carried us across that dark lake, and through even darker channels, to our cabin by 10:30 or so... But that cabin clearly spoke to us a welcome; in the Spirit only, but we both heard it... A snappy fire, a can of chili, and we snuggled into those warm bunks by midnight."

F. M. J., Thursday, September 2, 1965: "Oh what healing therapy in those simple bunks, in a simple cabin in the wilderness... A brilliant morning sun, slashing across the pond, had us up and ravenously enjoying an admittedly unorthodox breakfast of spaghetti and meat balls, heated in the cans over the fire... What silent, soothing, soul-filling peace, with yet that undercurrent of excitement that only immersion in the wilderness can provide...

"Lloyd played with a fish line awhile, and I sawed a willow off the outhouse, and cleaned up a mess an invading squirrel had made around the cooking area... We took a frigid swim, in the nude, in that northern pond, and reluctantly left about 3:00 P.M. His job was calling, the Copper Sands were calling. Such a very brief time. But I had been with my son.

F. M. J., Friday, September 3, 1965: "All up at 5:30; Lloyd ran us out to Anchorage International Airport; breakfast on the plane, and we were 'home' in Cordova before 8:00 A.M.

"We picked up and read our mail, paid bills, deposited checks, and received company all day—Jerry Baron and Dezzi Kamerer once, Rae Baxter and his wife, Sara, and baby daughter, Lynx, Carol Roys and Barbara Johnson, and then Bobbie Anderson, Jerry again, and Irving Warner in late with a six-pak of beer.

"We have stepped back through the veil into that other dimension, and that touching time with my son is now but a nostalgic and fragrant memory."

Prologue to Bering River

[I recognize that, in this "final story" that follows, there seems to be an evident shift in the style. Much of the writing is very subjective. But I do believe, that, if we can acknowledge that subjectivity, and accept it, we shall be carried into the intimacy, the inner heart of a man, far from home, and immersed in a brief, but unique life that few, very few, would *ever* have the opportunity to experience.

So read the simple statements of breakfasts, and steaks, and sleepy times, and engine repairs, and feelings, and longings; and, of introspective, personal observations. Read them, not as uninteresting, subjective observations, but see them as small, but clear windows, windows through which you, yourself, can intimately experience that most unusual, brief life, lived, so long ago, there, on the eastern edge of the copper sands. - Author.]

CHAPTER 26

Bering River

The Silvers

Both Sport, and old-time Commercial Fishermen tell me that Silver Salmon are the mavericks of the salmon clan. Other salmon are fairly predictable, but not the Silvers.

Sport fishermen tell me that they have been trolling for and catching Silver (Coho) salmon from just beneath the surface; and nearby, other Sport fishermen have been jigging for and catching them in great depths.

I know that I recall only a fraction of the stories that the Commercial fishermen told me, but here are a couple: "Silvers are smart, or determined. They will spawn almost anywhere—in the sand, or the mud, in the gravel, or even in the wetland grasses along the shore.

"And their determination?" they were saying, during a story telling time between fishing periods, "I tell you, they are determined.

"Four boats of us were fishing up a slough (and he named it). Yes, I know it is illegal to anchor our drift nets, but our leadlines were holding us all in place. We each were strung clear across that slough, a thousand feet, or yards, apart. The first boat should have been catching all the fish, but he wasn't. We were all catching about the same. Those fish just had to be burrowing into the mud to get by each net, some making it past the first, second, or third nets, and some not."

F. M. J., Saturday, September 4, 1965: "...My 46th birthday, but the Silvers of Bering River don't know, or care...

"Pulled out with the *Brant*, alone, at 3:45 this afternoon, to catch the tide across the flats... Anchored for the night behind the Copper Sands about 7:00. ...Beautiful, mostly cloudy day."

F. M. J., Sunday, September 5, 1965: "Weighed anchor about 9:00, with the Wx, W5 OVC 3LF, Wnd C. (Weather, indefinite ceiling 500 feet overcast, visibility 3 miles in drizzle and fog, wind calm.)

"Studied my chart, and then took a couple compass courses and got out into the Gulf OK. And then, navigating with but compass, fathometer, and clock, anchored up in Bering River 7 hours later. I could only rarely see the shore; and it got pretty rough as the wind picked up to SE, 20 to 25 knots. Still, a good trip...

"Lunch, visited with a few fishermen, and then took the skiff and took down the two markers there, as the new rules had to fit those Silvers..."

The Cop On The Beat

F. M. J., Monday, Sept. 6, 1965: "Up at 3:00 A.M.; dark, cloudy, rainy—and sleepy. Hot cup of tea, and then pulled out with my skiff in the barely perceptible dawn, and looked for possible fishermen jumping the gun. Back to the *Brant* about 4:30 for breakfast, and then cruised out to the bar and back, policing the opening time of 6:00 A.M.

"Pulled out for the east side (of Kanak Island) about 6:30, in weather, 500 feet overcast, visibility 2 miles or less in light drizzle and fog. Had to run compass to Okalee Channel, the east entrance.

"Lay on the east side, most of the day, talking to interesting fishermen.

"The weather started to clear about 3:00, so I pulled out for Okalee Spit; but a swiftly moving storm moved in by the time I exited the channel, with the weather, indefinite ceiling 500 feet overcast, visibility 1 mile or less in heavy rain and fog, and the wind SE 25 to 35 knots. So I turned for the west entrance. Had to run compass parallel to some of the hugest swells I've seen. We were half way in the west entrance before I was sure I was in it. A couple breakers nearly broached the *Brant*, and half swamped my skiff. That, plus dodging fishermen I could see only half the time, made the affair a busy and interesting time.

"Now, at 9:00 P.M., there is little evidence of the silence. No gentle patter, but rather a pounding of rain on the overhead and deck; no soothing sound of the surf, but an angry roar..."

A Night City

F. M. J., Tuesday, September 7, 1965: "Up early into a quiet, mostly cloudy day, and spent most of the day just patrolling the area with my skiff, and talking with fishermen. Heading out for the east side about 4:00 this afternoon, when Bob and Charlie Allen flew in. So I ran back inside so they could land, and talk, *and* eat my food. They left about 5:30, so I just anchored back in the main anchorage, ate my supper, and finished my book, *CONCORD REBEL*.

"It is so dark now, as I write this:

"It is so interesting what the night tells and shows us that we cannot see in the daytime, for all the light. In the day, there are just quite a number of boats, large and small, anchored here. But at night, we live in a city; quite mobile and fleeting, I agree, but still a city—the sounds of engines, and voices, and radios, traffic busying to and fro, lights marking well each abode; and occasionally the smells of fuel or exhaust; and all punctuated by the stillness, and darkness, and dampness of the night."

The Way, the Truth, and the Life

F. M. J., Wednesday, September 8, 1965: "It is now 10:00 P.M., and I try to review the day. Practically no wind all day, and in the stillness tonight, the distant surf has a soothing sound, as does the occasional, almost tinkling slap of tiny wavelets against the hull, or the flicker of flame in the fire pot on the stove.

"...Pulled out for the east side about 9:00 this morning for a *much* easier crossing of the bar. Tied to the tender, *Blue Bird*, for an hour, talking to fishermen, and watching fish transfer... The word is out that the season has been extended for another weekly period of 60 hours, starting next Monday at 6:00 A.M.; so it means another week away from home.

"What paradoxes we humans are, seeking, seeking, seeking, for peace, joy, and the vibrant vitality of life in ourselves and our immediate surroundings, and almost, but never quite finding our treasure.

"I wouldn't trade my present job for any that I know, or have even dreamed of; and yet it fails to produce, or perhaps more correctly, I fail to find the completeness in the romance that any dreamer of a life on the sea should correctly expect.

" 'I am the way, the truth, and the life...' and peace and joy. Why do we doggedly seek another way?

"...Rudy Becker brought me several flounders this evening, and then showed me how to skin and fillet them out with a few, deft motions with a sharp knife. I now have enough clear meat for a fine meal tomorrow...

"...Earlier in the day, I studied the most interesting, long streaks in the water, 10 to 20 inches wide, and 20 feet apart, formed by the silty, glacier water meeting the clearer ocean water. Stratus clouds in the water? Or the Master Painter playing with a lettering brush?"

To Tell the Story

F. M. J., Thursday, September 9, 1965: "I have observed that most people do 'something' wastefully far too often, because they cannot, or will not believe that they can do 'nothing' constructively, or with profit. The corn grows while the farmer is doing nothing about it. True, he must plant, cultivate, and harvest (as with man), but it *grows* while he is doing nothing about it. Is that not also the same with man? We must practice doing nothing for sufficient periods between the planting and the harvest, else there may be too little to harvest when the time is come.

"My alarm rang raucously at 5:00 A.M., but in my deeply, sleepy state, I couldn't imagine sufficient reason to go clam digging to draw me out of that snug and warm bunk. So I let it run down, and went back to sleep till nearly 8:30.

"This was another closed, no fishing, period in the week, so there was no pressure on me, other than a healthy hunger. So I cooked and ate my breakfast in that tiny but efficient galley, and looked out upon a lovely, partly cloudy day, though with a few fog banks to the west and south...

"Bob and Charlie dropped from the sky in the float plane about 9:00. I still have the two markers aboard that I had taken down, over on Bering River. Bob wants me to put them up between here and Cape Suckling. So later, I paddled my skiff ashore and cut some guy stakes.

"I must make more excursions ashore. There is a special, refreshing, restoring solitude in the wilderness that even the sea cannot provide. And occasionally, like periods of doing nothing, a man needs the solitude that only a complete immersion in nature can provide.

"Took my skiff over to the purser, *Alcor*, and visited awhile with Skipper Rudy Becker, and friend, Harold Hanson. No one had a large hammer, so I borrowed a piece of railroad iron with which to drive my stakes...

"Back aboard my own ship, I looked over that always amazingly long list of 'must do' items on the *Brant*, but couldn't find anything sufficiently pressing to inspire me to work. So I finished the huge, and delicious, Dungeness crab salad I had made yesterday, boiled the flounder fillets, and watched the fog roll in, and wrote a poem about it. It is a curiously structured poem, more like three, single verse poems strung together. But, it tells the story. And that is what I am compelled to do, tell the story.

"Our Own

The fog hangs low, and drifting, drifting swiftly
                      on the breeze;
the sky peaks through, and spreads its blue for
                      a moment on the sea.
The wavelets ring their tinkling bells against the hull;
and from the sky, comes the hungry cry of a lonely,
                      gliding gull.

Off my port bow,
two pursers hang on slanting scopes of anchor line.
The cluster of small boats attached speaks well
                          of wine,
but friendship too, and sharing of tall tales
of bigger hauls, and thicker fogs, and gales.

The flooding tide so soon will hide the sand
                          surrounding us;
and then will be but a tiny sea, with a wall of
                          mist, and thus
three tiny ships will find themselves, at anchor
                          and all alone,
in a world that I, with the mist and the sky
                          and solitude, call
our own.

                                      Aboard the M/V *Brant*
                                      Kanak Island, Alaska
                                      September 9, 1965"

To Mend the Cloak Again

F. M. J., Friday, September 10, 1965: "Had my alarm set yet again for 5:00 A.M., so I could get out and set one marker up on the low tide. But it was too foggy to even see Cape Suckling, so back to bed.

"Intermittent fog most of the day, with a few bursts of sun. So I sat in my cozy cabin, and spent the day, finishing up my end of month paper work...

"But it cleared enough by 4:30 and the afternoon low tide, for me to take the skiff and set one marker out a couple miles over toward Cape Suckling. It was dark by the time I returned at 7:00.

"Listened all evening to radio stations in Seattle and the Lower 48, 1500 to 2000 miles away. They were all loud and clear. I suppose radio engineers have an explanation for it, but that 6 inch by 12 inch by 16 inch box was giving me reception as if we were in the same town. What an incongruous world it is in which we live. The electronic wonder of radio has set me in an auditorium in Seattle, listening to Washington State Governor, Dan Evans, and at the touch of a switch, I am alone, thousands of miles away, hidden in an unnamed corner of a sand and water wilderness. Somehow, the touch of that switch intensifies the loneliness. Was that it? The closeness of those voices had torn a bit of the cloak away. I had some mending to do."

Balance Is the Thing

F. M. J., Saturday, September 11, 1965: "Had my alarm set yet again for 5:00 A.M., to try to get my last marker set out on the morning low tide. But yet again, the fog would not allow it.

"But later, it turned into a beautiful, still day, with a thin overcast that occasionally broke apart to reveal the bluest, blue sky. I weighed anchor about

9:00, and with my fathometer, felt my way up the Quintasol (often pronounced Quinasaw) channel, and tied alongside the *Thunderbird*, and the *Choctaw*, about 11:30.

"At their most hospitable invitation, I took my .30-06 rifle, and went ashore with the *Thunderbird* Skipper Fred Lange, Bobbie Anderson's step-father, and *Choctaw* Skipper Bob Ott, and Fred's two lovely children, Sylvia and Carol.

"We walked across Okalee Spit to the ocean side, over huge Brown Bear tracks (fresh), and hundreds of earthquake cracks from 2 to 6 inches wide. There were patches of brilliant Fireweed, and thousands of miniature field mouse, or Lemming trails. Watching closely, we could see them, but it was more like dark, gray streaks, running for their burrows a few feet ahead of us.

"We beachcombed the ocean side for awhile, and Fred found, and carried back, at least a 200-foot coil of plastic rope in quite good condition. I found a Russian steel fishing float, *and* my first glass ball fishing float. It was a beautiful, dusty blue from being blasted by the blowing sand. It had a small, but clear Japanese emblem, or identification mark on one side.

"When we reluctantly left the beachcombing, and returned to our boats, Fred's wife, Mae (who is Bobbie Anderson's mother), and Bob Ott's wife, Betty, had an excellent dinner of spaghetti and ground beef sauce ready for us aboard Fred's boat. They asked me to stay. The two women waited until we were finished, and then sat down themselves to eat.

"They had all been berry picking and clam digging last evening, so today had canned the blueberries, and were presently canning the clams in metal cans in pressure cookers. These people continue to add to their net income even during the closed fishing periods; and they do it so easily and casually. That radio link with Seattle: I think I will not listen tonight. The world will not go away, nor should it. But let me, Lord, rest in this healing balm for yet but a little while.

"We sat around in those warm cabins and talked, and drank coffee the rest of the day. This evening, on the low tide, Bob Ott rowed over to a bar with me and helped me put up my last marker. That marker would restrict even his fishing; but such was the character of this fine man, that I felt a real oneness with him. We just did what was best for the fishery; that was all.

"I cut loose from them just at dark, and ran off a hundred yards or so and dropped my own anchor for the night. There was not a breath of wind all day or tonight, and the stars and a huge, yellow moon are winning out over the clouds. This could be a pretty dangerously exposed anchorage, in any kind of a blow, especially at high tide; but right now, anchored in a pool in the sand, it is peaceful and beautiful, yet with that subtle undercurrent of excitement that makes this life so full.

"I think it is evident that I need other people more than I realized, because I was alone (no visiting) all day yesterday, and by this morning was getting low and blue and wondering what I was really doing out here alone and away from my family. But tonight, although I still miss my family, there is a fullness and richness to life. Balance is the thing; for each to find, and keep, the proper balance for himself between gregariousness and solitude. Too much of either means too little of the other; and like any extreme is an imbalance, and thus an eventually intolerable condition."

The Garden of the Sea

F. M. J., Sunday, September 12, 1965: "Weighed anchor about 9:00 in weather, indefinite ceiling 100 ft., sky obscured, visibility one-half mile in fog, and, with but my compass and fathometer, felt our way back to Kanak Island.

"What an experience, and what a contrast to Prince William Sound where one is cruising among the mountain tops. This is boating in the desert, with more sand than water, and where even some of the water is really only a thin film, and being that thin film of water, is less useable than the sand.

"Had a late breakfast, and then pulled out, about 11:30, into a clearing and increasingly beautiful day with not a whisper of a breeze. Anchored down on the west side a bit after 1:00. It was a *much* easier crossing of the bar; but several old veterans have told me, 'This bar is a mean one.'

"Read for awhile, and listened to my radio, and had lunch. And then I got itchy for a walk; so took my skiff over to the island, and hiked out for the outside beach.

"The time was 4:30, and low tide not until 7:30; but I saw a man, out by the surf, digging clams. So I started to walk out that way, and in a little bit, sure enough, clam holes.

"I didn't have my clam shovel, but I have heard that, although razor clams are well named, and firm contact with their edges will indeed slash the flesh, that they lay in the sand with those edges toward the sea. So I dropped to my knees and started digging, with my hands, parallel to the surf; and in 10 minutes had ten 7- or 8-inch clams. I probably could have cracked a safe with my sand-worn fingertips, but I already had my treasure. I carried them back in my shirt tail. [Pacific Coast razor clams, fried in butter: My mouth is watering now, as I write this.] Get these fellows fishing on the next open period in the morning, and I'd better go clam digging.

"Talked to Capt. Don Thornton on the *Chilkat*, on 2512, this morning. He was on his way to Valdez, and said he would check on my wife when he got back to Cordova tomorrow."

The Bright and the Dark Side

F. M. J., Monday, September 13, 1965: "4:30 A.M.— A brilliant, red sunrise out of the east that still seems north to me.

"Breakfast, and watched, and felt the activity and tension mount.

"5:30—Weighed anchor in a brisk east breeze, and strong ebb tide, and cruised down to the bar. Cabin skiffs were circling a pet spot like a mother bird hovering over a nest site, and saying, 'This is mine.'

"6:00 A.M.—My, what a good bunch of boys. The earliest to set was only three minutes early; very good.

"I ran out to the outer bar, and could have crossed easily, and on an ebb, and almost low water.

"Anchored back in the main anchorage, and took the skiff ashore on Kanak Island, and, with a clam shovel, and my pack sack, hiked a mile around to the ocean and dug 30 lbs of clams in about 45 minutes. Of course they increased to 50 lbs by the time I hiked them back to the skiff. What a contrast to Long Beach, Washington. Here, there is 10 miles of beach, and clams thicker than sand fleas, and not another soul in sight.

"The NE wind piped up, and by 11:30 was blowing 25–30 knots; and, with the strong flood tide, developed quite a sea, even here in the anchorage. The wind against the tide forced our boats to lie abeam of the chop and roll like peeled piling...

"Stopped, on one patrol, to talk to an old fisherman, Ed Gilbert, who gave a half hour lecture (not without considerable defense on my part, however) on what a stupid, blind, vindictive, etc., etc. S.O.B Ralph Pirtle was; 'And Rae Baxter is not much better.' It didn't phase him when I insisted that he was only one in 100 who felt that way. Those were some of the difficult moments in this job.

"...Well, this ____ rolling will bug us for an hour and a half before the tide changes and we can swing with the wind.

"7:30 P.M.—Well, the tide changed, and the rolling stopped; but not the wind. The tide is about to change again, so it looks like another 6 hours of rock and roll...

"...Cleaned all the broken clams, about 30, and hung the rest over the stern in a sack. Steam fried a dozen for dinner, and wrote more on a letter home... Hoped Bob and Charlie would fly in today to take it, and the clams home, but they didn't show." [I note a tug of disappointment at my heart, even now as I write, these long years later.]

The Ebb and Flood of Feeling

F. M. J., Tuesday, September 14, 1965: "Well! What a night. Up a dozen times battening things down, and securing the skiff alongside to keep it from pounding. Slept through the tide change, and before the waves subsided, they managed to fill the skiff; and at 3:30 A.M., I found it awash. The clamp was stuck on the motor, so I couldn't get it off; and with the strong ebb and waves, I couldn't gain on bailing; so I went back to bed.

"Up again at 7:00; the wind and tide had slacked off, so that I could bail out the skiff, and get the motor off. I had lost one oar, so after breakfast, I started up the *Brant*, and cruised down to the bar, looking for the oar, and checking the fleet.

"As I came back, the tide was flooding again, and the wind back up; it was too____ rough to anchor again out in the main anchorage, so I ran up above Point Hey to a little hole inside the sand, and next to the mountain, and anchored among half a dozen pursers, and a couple dozen cabin skiffs."

[Let me interject here, that, although this was not a purse seining operation this time, but was restricted to drift, or gill-net fishing, many who had them, brought their large purse seiners, towing their skiffs with them. Surely, the roomier, and sometimes almost yachtlike quarters on the larger boats, made the long stay away from home much more endurable. And often also, wives "kept house" while the men were out fishing.]

Continuing from my Journal: "My outboard motor wouldn't start, so I hauled it in, stripped it down as best I could, and hung it almost over the stove so it would dry out... Paddled the skiff over, in a real Autumn storm, to the large cabin skiff, *Choctaw*, for a jolly good time, for 3 hours, drinking coffee, swapping lies, and listening to the rain and wind.

"Paddled back 'home' about 4:30, and after packing that motor in and out several times, and finally heating the plugs on the stove, it started and ran fine.

"What a protected little anchorage this is. I can't get out (with the *Brant*) at low tide, and I can't see the actively fishing fleet from here; but there is none of that miserable rolling.

"What ebb and flood of feeling I have for this job. Last night and this morning, they 'could have had it.' But tonight, in a snug, warm cabin, in a smooth, protected anchorage, 'My cup runneth over.'

"8:15 P.M.—There most definitely is no pitching and rolling now, except that which the sailor feels for a time after coming ashore. I am so solidly aground I just walked alongside the boat, and could have walked around it. She's listing pretty much to port, but if I can *stay* in bed, I reckon I'll go...

"Only a breeze down where we are, but the roar of the wind up on the hill above us, is great for sleeping. I just walked out and carried the anchor around behind the boat, *and*, 30 feet closer to the water.

The Security of Our Fortress

F. M. J., Wednesday, September 15, 1965: "6:00 P.M.—Rain is thundering on the cabin, but there is only a light to occasionally brisk breeze down where we are. Up on the hill, however, the trees are occasionally whipped around by the 25 to 35 knot wind, that is also blowing out in the open anchorage.

"Slept in till 9:00, this morning, breakfast, on a slightly listing ship, and then we slipped off the sand about 10:30... Cloudy, with rain and wind picking up all day... Most of the skiffs fished the low water this morning, but it was getting too rough, so most were anchored in here by tonight...

"...The fishing period has been extended, again, until Saturday morning at 6:00; but we still don't know if the season will be extended beyond that.

"Cleaned up and shaved, and ran the skiff over to the *Choctaw*, and visited, and drank coffee, and listened to lies, and counter-lies with Bob Ott and his wife, Betty (after whose Indian Tribe they had named their boat). There was a continuing string of company, including Sam Jones, Sam Ott, Bob's son, 'Emmy' Carlson, and others.

"Surprisingly, about half did not smoke, and some did not drink, although most nipped the jug, and one drug at the bottle all day. But they all sincerely respected my refusal to drink on the job. Their language was pretty rough, even with Betty there; but somehow, it wasn't filthy, or even dirty. It was just earthy and took the baser functions of man as a matter of course.

"Frequently, of course, I was 'in a corner taking on all comers,' who wanted to take a poke, or two, or three, at the ADF&G. But essentially, it was a sporting, sparring match (though not always without some feeling), and in good humor. What an experience in human relations.

"At one time, there must have been ten or more in that 6' by 8' cabin, with Betty making, and pouring one pot of coffee after another. One by one, they finally all left, and Betty and I quietly shared. Maybe it was our common Indian blood that made us close, but we were good friends.

" 'The fellows like you, Nic,' she quietly announced.

"And I found myself answering, 'I really appreciate that, Betty, I really do; but you know, if I catch one of them fishing early, or fishing inside the markers, I'll nail them.'

"But her ready answer, 'Oh they know that Nic; they know that.' What a treasured compliment.

"Back to the *Brant* about 3:30, and ran down to a new cannery pickup ship, the *Moonlight Maid*, about a 110-footer looking more like a seagoing yacht. I was hoping to pick up stove oil, and bread and butter and sugar, but he could let me have only butter and sugar until his own supplies come in tomorrow. I hope I spell his name correctly, but the Captain, Gene Caforno, wouldn't take any money for the food. But we had quite a conversation on how the Fish and Game ought to be run, which seems to be 'par for the course.'

"It was really rough out there, with the wind blowing down the bay at 35 to 40 knots, and white caps rolling 3 to 4 feet. My little ship was really pitching, and taking spray over, on the way back up.

"Anchored more in amongst the fleet, this time, so I wouldn't go aground. This anchorage is so small that, with about 12 pursers, and 30 to 40 cabin skiffs, we all must anchor much closer than what would be considered good practice in a roomier place. There is one cluster of two pursers, and three skiffs, 50 feet off my port stern, and a cluster of seven or eight cabin skiffs, 75 ft off my port bow. At low tide, this slot in the sand can't be much over 150 ft wide, and 1500 to 1800 feet long.

"What is that keen excitement that subtly stirs us while lying at anchor in a good anchorage, on a dark night, with the rain beating vainly on the cabin top, and the wind roaring its futile threatenings through the trees up on the hill? True, the storms in their turn rule us, and sometimes bring fear almost to our lips. But now, we have the storm walled out, and we revel in the security of our fortress."

Weariness

F. M. J., Thursday, September 16, 1965: "I'm tired, and I want to go home. So much in the night that could, and should inspire to poetry of thought and expression, if not an outright poem. The stillness of motionless air, and dry though cloudy skies; the intense darkness jewelled by the lights of this miniature, floating city; the silence that is heard as a separate and distinct roar from the incessant roar of the ocean, that in itself neither sounds angry, nor soothing, but weary, as one who has fought a losing fight, but cannot yet concede defeat, even though the sand remains, and will yet remain for ages to come.

"It takes a vibrantly alive mind not so much to feel and be aware of the poetry of a night (the weariest soul, not asleep, can hear and love a symphony), but to put it into words that record it for others to hear and feel.

"I weary too easily. I know that I am no more a youth; but by the grace of God, I'm a long way from being an old man.

"...Up at 7:00, and took the skiff down through the fog to the bar to see if I might catch someone with an anchored net. No luck (either good or bad, depending on how one looks at it), so pulled the skiff ashore, down by the inside of the entrance, on the mainland side, and walked out to the ocean. No wind or rain, and the sun was peaking through and dissipating the fog.

"Dug one clam by hand, but it was small, so I put it back. Besides, I had my uniform on, and it is getting raunchy enough, just from wearing it.

Visited with a few fishermen on the way back to the *Brant*, and finally had my breakfast of the last of my ham (eggs long gone), and nearly the last of my stove oil.

"Weighed anchor at noon and ran down to the main anchorage, anchored over near Kanak Island, and changed oil and filter in my engine, and cleaned up the ship a bit.

"Bob and Charlie in with the floatplane, and stayed long enough to eat some of my dwindling food. Still, they took a letter back to my wife in Cordova.

"Ran down to the tender, *Copper King*, just in from Cordova, and filled my stove oil tank, and picked up some bread, and eggs, and meat... Should, or felt I should, take the skiff down to the bar looking for any anchored nets, but can't seem to muster the energy, or the initiative."

Only I Shall Remember

F. M. J., Friday, September 17, 1965: "Awake at 7:00, so up for breakfast of eggs again (even if a bit, uh, stale) and toast and tea. Good tea again, now that I have sugar.

"Real east wind storm again, so bundled up in my foul weather gear and took the skiff on patrol down to the bar and around. Hardly any swell on the bar. Someone had found my oar and had stood it on end in the sand; so I scooted ashore and ran up after it. I feel much safer now.

"Visited with fishermen on my way back up, then decided to go clam digging. There was a 5 foot holdup on the low tide; but by picking around, and digging carefully so as not to injure them, I got over 20 lbs. Back to the *Brant*, the tide was starting to flood, and the wind picking up, and the rock and roll starting, so weighed anchor and ran back up above Point Hey, and snuggled in amongst the re-grouping fleet again.

"Fishing is dropping off sharply, and when Charlie Allen and Rae Baxter dropped in in the floatplane, Rae said we'd know for sure tomorrow morning, but that it looked like this was the end of the season. I visited with them over on the *Linda Marnell*, Martin and Helen Anderson's small purser, and drank Helen's coffee, and ate her pie.

"Back to the *Brant*, and re-packed my stuffing box, and then fried up a package of delicious, sirloin steak that I had gotten from the *Copper King*.

I was out of clean clothes, so did a bit of laundry this evening, and made a walk-in clothes dryer out of this Official Patrol Boat for the State of Alaska, Department of Fish and Game.

"Ah, little anchorage; what friendship we have formed so soon. Tomorrow I must hie to the open sea, and leave your snug and protective arms. Oh yes, I want to go home, and your pleading and your promises will not detain me; but I shall miss you, little anchorage.

"The season should end tomorrow, and our little company, our town, our family of common interest will be no more. But tonight, with the rain and the warning of winter in the air, the rows of squared and lighted windows on the pursers strung out behind me, speak of coffee and good talk of the season past, and talk of plans for the coming winter. Little thought, and less talk will there be, in those warm cabins, of any anticipation of nostalgia concerning you. But I shall not forget.

"As the ebbing tide holds every boat pointed in the same direction, so the ending season points us all in one, common direction, home. But beyond that, our courses will be as variant as the points on a compass, and only I shall remember you and your kindness to us all."

The Party's Over

Or so we thought.

F. M. J., Saturday, September 18, 1965: "And here we are, back again in our little anchorage. And it is like saying the properly emotion-filled goodbyes to warm friends, and then finding that you must stay yet awhile. Sort of an anti-climax, a disappointment, an awkward and uncomfortable feeling; and no one knows what to say. We can't start up anew, yet the old is finished for this time.

"Up at 5:30 into a still, but thickly foggy day. Ran the *Brant* down to the bar and back to the main anchorage, putting in an official appearance, and, looking at the bar. No one was fishing, and those who fished the low water earlier caught very few.

"Breakfast and shaved, and then had company of fishermen until 2:00 P.M. All were wanting 'official' word that the season is closed—or extended. But we only *heard* that some 'Fish and Game people' were to fly down and do some test fishing, before a final determination is made. But it was too foggy for flying, so no one showed. Most boats were leaving anyway, and I can't blame them much; this not knowing is pretty hard to take.

"Cooked a huge T-bone steak for my lunch; took a short nap, and then eased the *Brant* back up to Point Hey. Took my skiff over to a cluster of big and little boats, and visited with waiting fishermen. I notice that I'm getting tired of defending the ADF&G.

"The chatter on the radios this evening is funny, and the bubbling excitement is like the windup of a construction job—The party's over; let's shout our goodbyes, and go home."

The "Earthen Vessel" Exposed

F. M. J., Sunday, September 19, 1965: "Well, finally, we get word that the season is indeed ended; and we get it through Barney Spielman. *No* official word direct to the ADF&G Agent in the area. To put it very, very mildly, it was damned embarrassing to have the fellows coming around for information, and I had none.

"Up at 7:00, and finally considering breakfast about 8:00, when Juan Pinto, a Filipino of Spanish and Chinese extraction, tied on with his skiff, seeking information on the season. He stayed, and talked.

"At 8:00 P.M. he was still talking. I finally fixed some grub about 2:00, which we both ate while he kept right on talking. I'm not sure if he was lonesome, or perhaps a little different; but he was quite interesting, and one of the most informed people I've ever known. It is just that 12 hours of anyone is quite a bit at one listening.

"A couple other men in about 5:00 for information, and stayed and visited, and drank coffee til 8:00 when we heard the *Judy I* talking to *Parks 19* (a Parks Cannery tender), who said he *heard* that the season was over.

"What a way to run a war. Bitterness? No. Just a bit of the 'earthen vessel' exposed."

Home

F. M. J., Monday, September 20, 1965: "Death came near today. Juan Pinto drowned in the combers, trying to leave Bering River; and although I knew him but one day, I feel as though I have lost someone very close. And there is that subtle searching into the deeper recesses of our minds for clues that we might have said or done something just a little bit different, and altered, just enough, this tragic course of events. That inscrutable Filipino, who looked the Chinese of his mother, who was a US citizen, and knew he must so remain, but who carried the burden of an unfulfillable longing to go back to his own people and help them rise from the 'slavery of political and religious corruption;' this highly educated man who, with his broad mind, was able to talk freely of racial prejudice, and yet who showed the weariness and strain of carrying the burden of truth and justice and love in the face of that prejudice; who carried with him the mental material, gathered through his years of study and observation, for two books on Communism that would not only have helped his people, but all who see hope in Communism, to see that evil for what it is; this simple fisherman, who was not simple, this lovely man is now with the Christ Whom he loved; and we have lost, for this short time on earth, a brother.

"Felt the current of excitement to go at 7:30, so up into a still, partly cloudy day to find the *Patty S.* making final preparations to depart, towing two skiffs. So I made my own, and followed them down to the bar, where they turned back.

"It was a wise decision, in view of the combers breaking clear across, and a *rough* crossing for the *Brant*. The only real trouble I had was my own fault. In the haste to go, I had forgotten that I had set the coffee pot back on the stove. As the *Brant* fell 15 feet or more, off that first comber, that coffee pot overturned. The cloud of steam fogged up my windows, so that I was steering blind, with compass only, for a short while; which was a pretty bad situation.

"Once outside, however, although the rollers coming in from our left were huge (fathometer varying 10 to 15 feet, and they looked like 20, sometimes), and it was a stand up, brace yourself ride for over 7 long hours, and the fog held visibility down to less than a mile or two for most of the way, there was no real problem, until entering the Strawberry entrance.

"And then for about 45 minutes there was a quite busy and tense time dodging huge combers, slamming directly on my port beam, and listening to that gasoline engine cut out every time she would heel hard to starboard.

"So I spoke aloud to that boat and engine. This was no facetious thing. I reminded them that I had done my best to care for them and their health, all these months. It was now their turn to carry me safely home. And that engine would always pick up again when she was level. But it was a little rough on the nerves, and brought a little sweat under the arms.

"...Caught Rudy Becker off Hartney Bay, and gave him back his railroad iron, and learned that the sea had taken Juan Pinto.

"Pulled into the dock in Cordova at 4:30, where Bobbie Anderson met me. We talked a bit; and then he drove me home.

A Captain Without a Ship

We spent a few days letting the coiled springs unwind, and settling into the rhythm of the land. The year's fishing was ended; there was no more work for the *Brant*, and so:

F. M. J., Friday, September 24, 1965: "A beautiful day... Down to the boat at 8:00, and took the aerial mast down, and the chimney off the oil stove. Capt. Curran towed us to the oil dock for topping off her tanks, and then on to the Orca cannery, where we were to lay her up for the winter.

"We lifted her out, scrubbed down her bottom, drained the water, sprayed the ignition, and did the many, little jobs that prepared her for a long layup. Capt. Harry left about 3:00; and I stayed and stowed her ropes, worked at my final reports, and then ran my skiff back to Cordova about 4:00"

I don't remember my emotions at the time, but knowing my own nature, I know that I allowed some dampness around the edges of my eyes, as there is at this writing, patted her gently, and told her, "Rest well, my faithful friend, rest well in your long winter sleep," and then just walked away.

I was now a Captain without a ship—this is a story of the sea.

Epilogue

I still had a little over a month of my contract to fulfill; Bobbie needed a month's vacation.

So I was made *the* Protection Officer (Game Warden) for the month, policing the bear, deer, and fall bird hunting. There were some most interesting stories during that time. But I think I shall go now, and tell no more.

My heart and mind cannot speak more of the land. Rather, let us just rest for awhile, in the pleasant and nostalgic memories of one small ship and the sea; and let us breath, for yet a little longer, that pervading, sweet aroma of the Spirit of the Copper Sands.

Dean Nichols
Capt. M/V *Brant*

www.ingramcontent.com/pod-product-compliance
Lightning Source LLC
Chambersburg PA
CBHW060604230426
43670CB00011B/1955